CW00820193

Carl Theodor Dreyer and *Ordet*

Carl Theodor Dreyer and *Ordet*

My Summer with the Danish Filmmaker

Jan Wahl

UNIVERSITY PRESS OF KENTUCKY

The University Press of Kentucky

Scholarly publisher for the Commonwealth,
serving Bellarmine University, Berea College, Centre
College of Kentucky, Eastern Kentucky University,
The Filson Historical Society, Georgetown College,
Kentucky Historical Society, Kentucky State University,
Morehead State University, Murray State University,
Northern Kentucky University, Transylvania University,
University of Kentucky, University of Louisville,
and Western Kentucky University.
All rights reserved.

Editorial and Sales Offices: The University Press of Kentucky
663 South Limestone Street, Lexington, Kentucky 40508-4008
www.kentuckypress.com

16 15 14 13 12   5 4 3 2 1

Library of Congress Cataloging-in-Publication Data

Wahl, Jan.
  Carl Theodor Dreyer and Ordet : my summer with the Danish filmmaker /
Jan Wahl.
    p.   cm.
  Includes bibliographical references and index.
  ISBN 978-0-8131-3618-9 (hardcover : alk. paper) —
  ISBN 978-0-8131-3620-2 (ebook)
  1. Ordet (Motion picture) 2. Dreyer, Carl Theodor, 1889–1968.
3. Wahl, Jan. I. Title.
  PN1997.O73W34 2012
  791.4302'33092—dc23

                              2012003582

This book is printed on acid-free paper meeting
the requirements of the American National Standard
for Permanence in Paper for Printed Library Materials.

Manufactured in the United States of America.

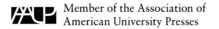 Member of the Association of
American University Presses

To Jean Drum,
Poul Malmkjaer,
and Ib Monty

Demain sera beau, disait le naufragé.
—Georges Rouault

Love can do all but raise the dead.
—Emily Dickinson

Contents

Illustrations follow page 86

Preface

This is an impressionistic yet detailed account of what was to be the most significant season of my life—that faraway summer of 1954. It took a half century to gain a true perspective on that unique experience, for when you are very young, you assume golden opportunities lie around every corner.

I was an American student on a Fulbright scholarship at the University of Copenhagen when Carl Theodor Dreyer graciously invited me to partake of a particular Danish summer—the summer he was to direct his now classic film *Ordet* (*The Word*), which was nominated for an Oscar and won the Golden Lion at the Venice Film Festival in September 1955, the Golden Globe from the Hollywood Foreign Press Association, the Critics Prize in Helsinki, and the Bodil (the highest Danish award) for Dreyer and for cameraman Henning Bendtsen. Dreyer planned to do outdoor shooting in Jutland, that portion of Denmark growing out of the mainland of Germany. The rest of the country—a "little land," as the Danes like to call it—is a series of some three hundred islands, including Sealand, site of the capital of Copenhagen.

Luckily, I saved my journals; every night I would write the happenings of the day. I also kept the transcriptions from the many conversations I had with Dreyer, a saintly, soft-spoken human being.

In addition, I have those corrections he painstakingly made in precise blue ink. All quotes from Herr Dreyer are his own words. The pictures are from Palladium Films and from Dreyer himself, who had faith that one day I would do a book.

How did I happen to win an unbelievable opportunity of watching the one and only Carl Theodor Dreyer at work on his *Ordet*? And what was this man like in offscreen life? How did he work and think?

I hope this little book gives some answers.

Special thanks must go to Lars Ølgaard from the Danish Film Institute and to Jean Drum, coauthor with her late husband, Dale, of *My Only Great Passion*, the remarkable study of Dreyer. Most of all, I wish to thank my good and faithful friend David Shepard, who has been constantly encouraging.

Introduction

As a child, I was taken to a revival of Charlie Chaplin's feature *The Gold Rush*. It had no talking, although in this version, Chaplin himself narrated. The bun dance enchanted me; suddenly I was aware that a totally different kind of film existed besides those with Betty Grable and Tyrone Power. Therefore, I elected to dip into the history of movies.

The public library in Toledo, Ohio, had a first edition of Paul Rotha's *The Film Till Now*. The stills from *Caligari* were thrilling. Only a handful of older films were available through the Museum of Modern Art and various rental agencies or, occasionally, by purchase. As I took the reels in my hands, running them on a 16mm Bell & Howell projector, I felt attracted to another great master—the Dane Carl Theodor Dreyer.

I located his Joan of Arc film in a cut-down version from Reed & Reed Distributors in Brooklyn. Even in this shortened print I could recognize the overpowering beauty of his images.

What had Dreyer dared to do? He peeled away the plaster and gilt and legend of the Maid of Orleans, which had suffocated her for centuries. This was not blasphemy but a penetrating look into the inner being with true art.

In 1927 Dreyer rebuilt, in the style of Giotto, old Rouen, with its churches and moats and towers; he brought in Bishop Cauchon and the other Inquisitors to light the faggots. Then he burned Joan of Arc once more at the stake.

The reality of *The Passion of Joan of Arc* was so palpable that in 1929, five hundred years after the actual event, when this amazing cinematic attempt to probe into layers of the past—stripping a historic occurrence bare—was shown in New York City, two spectators died in their seats from shock during the first week. Showings were canceled. The Catholic Church demanded whole scenes be excised from the film, although Dreyer had followed faithfully the transcripts from the original trial.

When I received my scholarship to the University of Copenhagen, I was pleased to know Dreyer was nearby. Besides, I began a love affair with that city the minute I stepped onshore. The school year seemed endless. Winter was like being in a pewter pot with the lid on.

People in Copenhagen have a way of celebrating spring and the sun. They enter Tivoli Gardens as soon as the sun breaks through the gray clouds, sit at one of the outdoor cafés, and order Tuborg beer with cold shrimp on buttered bread. Around this time also, forests filled with beech trees burst into bloom. Wood anemones and green things galore spread out over soft, velvety grass. Swans swim in the moats. The population begins to move out into the countryside. On the Sound, sailboats appear, and red-capped students with rucksacks and cameras pedal the roads. The old copper roof atop Elsinore Castle shines almost clear across the water to Sweden. Little children watch the skies for storks returning from Africa. Winter's lid has been removed; Danish hearts are buoyant.

It was in such favorable weather in 1954 that Dreyer was about to commence a new feature film, his first in nearly a decade and his first in his own small country since *Day of Wrath,* which was made during the Nazi occupation in World War II.

The previous November, someone I knew had glimpsed Dreyer at one of the fish restaurants along the canal in Copenhagen the evening before he was to fly to London to seek backing from J. Arthur Rank for the biggest project of his career. Dreyer was expecting to do a film on the life of Jesus and had already spent years on the manuscript and on planning, to the last detail, just what he needed. But he returned unsuccessful.

Herr Dreyer said that after World War II, producers in several countries urged him to come and start a film—but because of recent political history, he had no desire to do it. "When you have seen someone try to crush your country," he declared, "you cannot forget in a year or so."

Fortunately, he was not destined to suffer for his probity. At last the Danish government awarded him—as an international artist and a faithful Dane—the directorship of the Dagmar Theater, one of the country's most splendid moving picture theaters. The actor-director Benjamin Christensen, whose *Witchcraft through the Ages* had won him fame in 1921, and who later followed its success to Hollywood, where he fashioned offbeat features such as *Seven Footprints to Satan,* was similarly honored with a family cinema just outside Copenhagen.

Under Dreyer's guidance, the Dagmar showed the public Jean Renoir's *The River,* John Huston's *Moulin Rouge,* the Japanese *Rashomon* and *Gate of Hell,* and the American *The Little Fugitive* and *Carmen Jones.*

After November 1953, there were rumors printed in the newspapers saying that Dreyer might do a new film, a Danish one. Many didn't believe it. Knowing him to be uncompromising, they felt he would make no film until he found the means to begin his Jesus project. Why should he, it seemed on the spur of the moment, give up *The Life of Jesus?*

In the early spring of 1954, the headlines declared the film was to be *The Word,* from the mystical play *Ordet* by the martyred poet-vicar Kaj Munk. A puzzlement: the esteemed Swedish director Gustav Molander had already made a version in 1943.

Two years before I came to Denmark I had written to Dreyer, asking if he could help me secure a print of *Vampyr,* which he did. I sent him a message that I was now enrolled at the university and, through my adviser, Erik Saxdorff, was studying film courtesy of the Danish Film Museum.

In June, Dreyer telephoned to say that he and his wife

were renting a summer place at Rungsted, a small town on the coast between Copenhagen and Elsinore. Would I care to come up for tea and discuss the new film?

Without hesitation, I replied that I could leave at once.

1 Pastries at Rungsted

When I arrived, the day was shining. The Dreyers were staying at a modest painted house on a low hill surrounded by a yellow-green, abundant, leafy garden. I went up the round stone steps to ring the bell. Carl Theodor Dreyer opened the door himself, remarking gently, "The sun has come to light your visit."

In the hallway he informed me that his wife, Ebba, was absent, buying cakes and cookies for us at the bakery, and would soon be back; perhaps we could wait for her in the parlor. He led me in.

Nowhere in the house did I find the signs of movie preparation one might expect. No paper, pens, ink, typewriter. I saw nothing of model sets or sketches or books. The house was spotless, filled with fresh flowers. The windows and the back door were open. "I am busy at work," Dreyer said smiling, tapping his forehead.

We sat in the parlor. Herr Dreyer offered a cigarette, then looked at me eagerly. "Did you see *Limelight*?" he asked. I answered yes; the film had played in Copenhagen for six months.

"I learned much about poetic unity from Chaplin. As you might move in a museum, from one Rembrandt to another, seeing the essential harmony but having the sense of exploring depths that were unknown to you before, I could see both *The Kid* and *Limelight* on the same afternoon. Like Paul Klee too, he invents all the time. *Shoulder Arms* and *The Great Dictator*, I think, are the best documents we have against war. It was wonderful to have the war in the trenches in *Shoulder Arms* represented as a bad dream the Tramp was having."

Dreyer said he could still hum the theme from *Monsieur Verdoux* and did so. It was a sinister, satirical Viennese waltz. I proceeded to whistle the irresistible dance of the shadow people from *Vampyr*; the German composer Wolfgang Zeller had written the score for Dreyer's film.

"Yes, I am fond of it also," he admitted. Then he suggested that we carry two lawn chairs out into the garden. "In Denmark we learn to drink up every bit of the sunshine." Once we were sitting outside, he said: "Now I want to ask what you think of Poul Schierbeck's music in *Day of Wrath*."

Day of Wrath deals with religious hypocrisy and witch-burning in the seventeenth century. The opening is direct and ominous—with no titles but the unrolling of a decree of death for Herlof's Marte, a foolish, harmless old woman who brews herbs. When a large number of farm sheep die, she is suspected and judged to be a witch. As the scroll unwinds, a massive organ-like orchestration of "Dies Irae" is played. The music ceases.

Next we are shown two women in a hut, bent over a steaming kettle; one of them mutters, "Water from the gallow's bank." Suddenly in the distance a witch-bell is heard, and a crowd chants the name of Herlof's Marte. She stands up stiffly, with a kind of fatalistic dignity. The bell rings incessantly, coming closer—it keeps on tolling. The music, used sparingly in *Day of Wrath*, is powerful and somber, rather Bach-like.

I replied that I found the music extremely suitable. "You know," Dreyer mused, "I promised Poul Schierbeck after we finished *Day of Wrath* if I ever did another film in Denmark he must again write the music. And so he is indeed, for *The Word*."

"Isn't that impossible?" I protested. "Schierbeck is dead."

"Yes. But I shall still keep the promise. His widow is giving me his unpublished manuscripts. From them I'll fit a score together. His music is just right for *The Word*."

I asked Dreyer if he planned to make *The Word* a contemporary piece.

"Well, I shall keep it in the time in which Kaj Munk wrote it; in other words, 1925. However, since it occurs out in the country, which is always touched less by the whim of fashion, its people will wear those dresses or suits which are timeless and rustic."

Then Dreyer's wife appeared. At the door she made a

signal with her hand. Dreyer rose from his chair. "It's the telephone," he explained. "It must have sounded as she came in." He excused himself and entered the house.

Fru Dreyer was fashioned like graceful Dresden china. "We shall have tea in a minute," she said, as I helped her with her parcels. "The studio has called. They want to know what color to paint the farmhouse kitchen. I am sure he wants it yellow. You cannot get away from such matters, even out here in Rungsted. Oh," she whispered, taking off her bonnet, "I hope for his sake the weather stays nice. He is going to make the outdoor scenes at Vedersø in Jutland, where Kaj Munk lived."

After Dreyer's return, he consulted his watch. "I have a visitor every afternoon at three-thirty," he declared. Soon after, a gray bird flew down and walked over to the back terrace, where we were sitting. Dreyer then broke up a cake into small pieces and flung them out into the grass.

The bird regarded us with a cool, steady eye and ate the crumbs—finally giving us a look of thanks and sweeping up into the air again. "Yes, it's the same one," Fru Dreyer laughed. "She has a black patch on her left wing."

"Do you think it is a she?" her husband asked. "Well, it must be—since she eats everything herself, leaving nothing to take home!"

As Fru Dreyer poured more tea, she announced, "Do you know, I was thinking of Maria Falconetti this afternoon. We were so much in love with her."

I asked if it was true that MGM had once (Dreyer later showed me the wire: it was 1938) suggested he remake *The Passion of Joan of Arc* with Garbo. He replied that it was so.

"But I told them once you have made something the way you want it, you don't repeat it. Falconetti gave herself up entirely to the personality of Jeanne d'Arc. She did not *act* it—she *was* Jeanne, completely. That is the difference between theater and film. It's all in the close-up. That is the give-away."

He continued. "Don't misunderstand me. Perhaps Greta Garbo could have done it. Even in her first films when she was a child, she knew how to respond intelligently to a camera. For instance, in Pabst's *The Joyless Street*, where Werner Krauss and Asta Nielsen, admirable as they are, cloaked themselves in the pompous air of theater, Greta Garbo was content to show the great purity of her personality alone."

In Pabst's German-made film from 1925, there's a touching sequence: Garbo is a young girl whose family in postwar Vienna is nearly starving; she goes into the office of a brothel keeper, offering to sell herself.

After I described that scene, Dreyer added, "Yes, you can *believe* in her humility and desperation."

Then we returned to Falconetti. Fru Dreyer said, "Her tastes varied; she would do a heavy drama one week and *Juliette, or The Key of Dreams* the next."

"So many people have thought," Dreyer explained, "that Falconetti was 'unknown' when I used her in *Jeanne d'Arc*. She was not; she was famous and well esteemed. She had a luxurious apartment on the Champs Elysées.

"But I talked to her, and she had faith in our project. She exercised a prima donna's temper just a few times—or [and his eyes twinkled] you might call it woman's vanity. It was in her contract that she agreed to have her hair clipped off in one of the scenes. But when the day arrived, the camera ready, she protested. She said, 'I will not do it.' She wept. I pleaded with her; I told her we had to have the real thing, that she must suffer it. After all, Jeanne did.

"That calmed her a bit, and we started the scene." Dreyer paused, then continued. "The man came up to her with the shears. She became hysterical, but I insisted and finally she gave way. 'All right,' she said. And we shot the scene."

The film concentrates solely on the merciless trial and burning of the peasant child who declares she hears voices. I added that I could imagine Elisabeth Bergner (for whom an adoring James Matthew Barrie wrote *The Boy David* in 1936 in London) dressed in armor, leading the French army. But this is not the Joan that Dreyer dealt with.

He acknowledged there was room for multiple interpretations, adding, "All inspirations must spring from the same source. She was honest and naïve. She must be treated that way.

"Now—Ingrid Bergman is a very fine woman and has much talent. However, she was not right for the role, just as she was not right in *For Whom the Bell Tolls*. Because no matter what you say, Bergman is too much a product of modern culture and civilization to portray a primitive peasant girl."

We finished the last of the whipped cream pastries. Before Fru Dreyer took the tea tray inside, she said, "During the war, Falconetti, Louis Jouvet, and others went to South America to perform. She soon fell upon hard times. She ended up opening a drama school to make her living but only got a few pupils." Her husband added, "Falconetti died there. She was our friend."

It was nearly the hour for my train. Dreyer telephoned the station to check its exact arrival time.

"I shall be leaving for Vedersø in two weeks," he informed me. "The interiors will be completed in the Copenhagen studios by then, so that when we finish with the outdoor scenes in Jutland, there will be no delay. We'll go directly into the interiors.

"In May, Fru Kaj Munk went with me to Jutland, helping to find 'motifs.' We would choose two or three sites for each, talking over the points every night until midnight. All the platforms and camera tracks have been set up and tried. Things should go quickly if the weather is good."

There was no sound from outside the house. Through the window, mellow Danish, early-evening summer's light filled the trees and grass with a soft, luminous yellow-green glow.

Herr Dreyer sat with me in the parlor. "I discussed," he said, "my script for *The Word* with Fru Munk. I wanted to be certain she felt it was true to Kaj Munk's spirit. I made changes, of course, because this is a film, not a play.

"When I first saw *The Word* performed, I wrote Kaj Munk, asking if he would care to sell the rights. He replied, humorously, yes, he'd sell—for two hundred fifty thousand kroner. So I have had to wait until the circumstances were right.

"In a way, this will be an 'in-between' experience for me. I want to see how people will react to a miracle, since the

Christ film will be full of them. I think this will help prepare audiences for seeing him, too, on the screen. The opening of the Book of the Evangelist says: 'In the beginning was the Word, and the Word was with God, and the Word was God.'

"You will recall that John, when he was not preaching, was sometimes mistaken for Jesus. In Danish, John is called Johannes. Munk's story in *The Word* tells of a divinity student who, in that period of intense study just before examinations, has suffered a mental collapse. He thereupon assumes the identity of Jesus.

"Consequently, this young man, named Johannes, thinks he can work miracles. He tries to raise a young woman in his family from the dead—as Jesus had spoken unto the corpse of the daughter of Jairus. 'Talitha cumi: I say unto thee, arise.' His attempt fails. Johannes forgot to ask God for the power. It comes as a great shock to him.

"His sane mind is restored to him, young Inger yet in her coffin. With a pure mind, he asks again for a miracle to occur: for her to wake. It is a question of faith. Johannes still believes. The girl comes alive and sits bolt upright in her coffin."

At the conclusion of this narrative, we sat for a moment in silence. Perhaps it was an effect from the light, but while he was speaking, his enthusiasm grew. The faint blue color in Dreyer's eyes seemed to leave altogether; they became an intense white, as if you could see through to the fire-hot vision burning in his head.

"This is a theme," he said quietly, "that suits me—Faith's triumph in the skeptical twentieth century over Science and Rationalism.

"And now," he said in a different tone, smiling, "we must go find my wife in the kitchen before you take your train."

In the second week of July, I received a simple postcard from Carl Th. Dreyer in Jutland, inviting me to attend the shooting. Since he ordinarily worked with a strictly closed set, I didn't hesitate. The school term was over—I was free for the remainder of the summer.

As I boarded the early ferry train crowded with expectant holiday-goers bound for the country and the seashore, I noticed the sky was clouded over. After a few hours, heavy, unceasing rains fell.

It's possible to travel from one end of Denmark to the other in less than half a day—as I was doing—from eastern Sealand to western Jutland. If I had booked a seat on one of the lightning trains, it would have been possible to accomplish the journey in several hours. However, now I had time to review in my mind the course of Dreyer's artistic career, so I traveled on two journeys simultaneously, with *The Word* forming the destination of each.

2 Small room with a view

Vedersø is located in a remote part of Jutland, which sticks up from Germany like a rather large thumb. To reach it, I took a series of trains with a boat in between—coming to the last part of the trip by bus. That is, I arrived as far as the village of Ulfborg, where there was a travelers' inn. Carl Th. Dreyer and his company had used up every spare room in the vicinity of Vedersø. I'd left Copenhagen on the island of Sealand, crossing the tiny island of Fyn (going through Hans Christian Andersen's birthplace of Ødense), and coming at last to the peninsula of Jutland.

The Denmark known to most of the world is a composite of many islands. Every inch of space is made interesting. There are little fishing harbors with painted houses and wide nets spread out to dry, elfin hideaways and beech forests, and the King's Deer Park at Klampenborg. The baroque, noble, splendid city of Copenhagen is full of spires and sharply slanted roofs, a network of delicate parks and busy canals, and bicycles that appear in full force in late afternoon. Tivoli Gardens has a fireworks display at midnight that sends explosions of color into the sky. Outside the city are workers' suburbs with modern apartment houses and active playgrounds. In the countryside, next to the clean roads, lie handsome cultivated farms—some houses wearing thatched roofs. A few abandoned windmills relieve the vast plane of flat landscape. A decade after World War II, Denmark hadn't changed much.

I was told that during World War I, however, a real change of spirit did occur. On a late summer's night, most of Copenhagen had walked down to the harbor at Langelinie to bid farewell to the small, gallant navy. One by one, the boats slipped away from the Sound, heading out to open sea. The people stayed until the last boat disappeared from view. Most of the fleet never returned.

In World War II, Denmark was quickly conquered by the German invaders. The heroic story of Danes one night taking the Jews across to Sweden by fishing boats to safety is well known. It speaks to the courage of the inhabitants of this special "little land." Generally, Danes keep a cheerful mien. They demand their social rights, and they are famous for wanting to live in reasonable comfort.

But the *stimmung* of Jutland in many respects is different from the rest of Denmark. For one, the terrain is more difficult. Long ago, the great oak forests that covered Jutland got chopped down to build Viking ships, leaving the unprotected land to be whipped by the North Sea and beaten by the strong winds.

The land fell to waste, becoming a lonely, sparse area of heath and moors and fjords. Still, the people clung to it and managed to grow simple crops. On the coast, every farmer also became a fisherman, and these two occupations fed the families.

A significant advance in the last century has been a growing movement to reclaim parts of the land and make the soil usable. This is done by marking off a large section of loamy ground and planting fir trees. Such a section is called a *plantage*, or planting place.

Twenty-five to fifty years later, there is a full-grown evergreen forest. It is then possible to remove some firs, leaving others as shelter, and to grow rye and barley. One generation's labor is carried on to the next—the end is not yet in sight. On my first evening in Ulfborg, I was encouraged by visiting the endless *plantage* outside the village.

The following morning, when I awoke at six, the sun was peering through a sky that was rimmed with thick, swollen clouds. The air was chilly. I set out with a pocketful of crullers, my midmorning snack. Dreyer had sent a message to meet him for *middag* at the Vedersø Hotel. Vedersø was several hours' distance by foot. The farmhouses I saw (which were few), unlike the village houses with red tile roofs, were thatched and sodded. Pots of plants sat at the windows. Beside the homes, flower or vegetable gardens were arranged with the delicacy of Japanese art.

Most of the land was rough pasture. Spotted and red cows and black and brown horses grazed side by side. Very little here was turned to cultivation. Midway, outside a crossroads called Staby, children flew a kite in the breeze. Four cars and two trucks eventually passed. I saw one stork. A winding lane took me from Staby to Vedersø.

Vedersø was only a hamlet; it consisted of a garage, a main store, and not much else. Kaj Munk's church sat on a slight incline and was closed in with a white picket fence. The church was whitewashed, like all old Danish country churches, and was built in the shape of a cross. It dated from the twelfth century and had escaped the wrath of Martin Luther. Its main section had been built under Bishop Absalon, who founded Copenhagen.

The church was of the simplest kind: a raised loft lay at one end, next to the entrance. The pulpit, baptismal bowl, and altar lay at the other. It seated about one hundred fifty souls. An adjoining room had been added on a few centuries later, with a small window carved in the connecting wall so worshippers might catch sight of the baptismal bowl. A ship's model hung by wires from the high ceiling. It seemed to me, as I stood in the empty church, that when Kaj Munk preached there, shouting out in anger against the Nazis, the wires must have vibrated—stirring into motion the little ship of Denmark.

"Did you see it?" Herr Dreyer asked, leading me onto the porch of the Vedersø Klit Hotel. "A ray of sunlight through the black!" We sat at a table and ordered morning coffee. "I arrived last Wednesday," he informed me. "In one week we have gotten only three single scenes—just linking shots." He stirred his cup, and his eye had a twinkle. "And I fear one of them—a wagon filled with rye, rolling across a bridge, shot looking upward from the bed of a stream, is almost too beautiful to remain in the film."

He sighed. "You know, we have to wait a day or two always before we can see the day's work. The film has to be put on the train at Ulfborg and developed at the laboratory in Copenhagen, then returned here, and we view it at the little cinema at Ulfborg. Meanwhile, we go about waiting for good weather and planning new shooting.

"Now we must get you a room here," he continued. "I have to stay in the annex myself, back behind, without heat. The furniture in my room is bright pink and I have to shut my eyes. Several people are less fortunate—being changed daily from the hotel to what private rooms we can manage nearby. I have heard, however, some vacationers are moving out. They have looked forward all year to swimming, I suppose; then they find this."

He scanned the dull, gray sky. He pointed to the puddles of water left on the gravel in front of the windows. A small gray truck was labeled PALLADIUM. Behind it, around the corner, lay an unhitched trailer containing the sound equipment. Aside from that and two or three cars, the place was deserted.

"Do you know," said Dreyer, "when Kaj Munk was five years old, a young mason in his village died. Little Kaj went out to his garden behind the house and prayed for the man to rise up out of his coffin. He believed in miracles, as children can.

"To me, the best believers are the child and the deranged person, since their minds are not rational and limited by proof-positive facts like ours. They have the sweep of a wider universe—where such things are possible. Who can say our normal everyday world is the only one? Little Kaj Munk's miracle failed—but must have preyed on his mind in some way or other the rest of his life.

"Kaj Munk and I have something in common: we were both orphans. His teachers were priests. In particular, his mother was very religious, and it was she who chose his occupation for him. He became pastor of the church at Vedersø thirty years ago. He wrote his plays all the while and sent them to the Royal Theater of Copenhagen. Getting no answer from the theater, Munk complained to a critic, who advised the impatient playwright to go home to write a play about Danish farmers. He did. He wrote *The Word* in six days.

"In the manuscript, I have cut out any reference to 'Grundtvigianism' and 'Jesus Mission,' known only to Danes. So the two opposing sects in the film will be known instead as the Glad Christians, led by old Morten Borgen, owner of the big farm called Borgensgaard, and the Sour-faced ones, led by the fanatic, puritanical village tailor Peter.

"The whole point of the play is in the miracle. So I have also omitted Munk's 'back door'—that is to say, in the second version of the play after the young woman Inger has raised up in her coffin, Munk has the Doctor complain that a faulty death certificate had been issued.

"True enough, the Doctor is intended as an unbeliever. But in such a film, you cannot turn ambiguous here. If the miracle is not genuine, then the play has no meaning."

We went outside to study the sky. No real change was

in sight, although a sharp wind blew. "Do you like candy?" Dreyer asked. "Have one of these—from the milk of cows herded high up on the mountains of Norway, where the sweetest grass grows. It makes the finest milk chocolate."

3   Sardines and cigars

Before lunch, we took a walk over the dunes to the North Sea, which crashed upon the shore some hundred yards behind the hotel. Walls of concrete helped keep the protective dunes from blowing away. There were several large pillboxes left as souvenirs from the Nazi occupation.

"Imagine," said Dreyer, "a strong, loving father like old Borgen who is disappointed by his three sons. The oldest, Mikkel, though he has a fine wife, Inger, and two small daughters, lacks the faith of the father. The youngest, Anders, has fallen in love with Anne, daughter of Peter Tailor—that is a crushing blow to the old man. And Johannes, the other son, in whom he had the highest hopes, for he shared his father's belief, has become deranged. Old Borgen, the Glad Christian himself, becomes filled with doubt."

He continued: "From the character of the man Johannes, the film will find its true style. I must pour into *The Word* an atmosphere in which a miracle is possible, keeping it, meantime, in touch with the Everyday. Life—*Life* must be the watchword."

Far out on the water we saw two fishing boats battling the waves. Dreyer climbed a dune. Like spilled gold, a patch of sunshine lit a distant rye field; the sky was still lowering. The gold was suddenly shut out, and we headed back to the hotel.

Dreyer's company occupied three full sides at the simple, long board tables of the dining room. An enlarged photograph of Kaj Munk hung on the wall. Preben Lerdorff, who had played the son Martin in *Day of Wrath* and would now play Johannes, entered and shook hands. He was a startling image of the bearded Christ as we know Him in paintings. He wore rough boots and a thick wool pullover.

I was placed at Dreyer's left; on the other side sat the grand old actor from the Royal Theater, Henrik Malberg, now in his eighties. At first, Herr Dreyer had considered Benjamin Christensen for the part of old Borgen. But Malberg's "mentality," as Dreyer put it, made him the inevitable choice. "That is how you feel someone is right for the role and you will see how he transforms himself until he is the living Borgen."

Henrik Malberg leaned forward to pass me sardines from Portugal. "These are real jewels," he declared. "But the greatest jewel for me you can't guess. Kaj Munk wrote *The Word* with me in mind for the part of Borgen. However, the Royal Theater, to which I was under contract, turned down the play on the grounds that *The Word* demands an *intimate* audience, and the Royal Theater seats sixteen hundred. When a small, intimate theater in Copenhagen, the Betty Nansen, agreed to do the play, the Royal Theater would not release me. To this day I have been unhappy over the affair; I felt cheated and regard this opportunity of playing Borgen as a personal triumph. So we must celebrate. Please have one of my sardines!"

I took it upon myself to mention the Gustav Molander version. Dreyer's only comment was, turning in the direction of the North Sea and the dunes: "This is what we in Denmark missed in it. He made *The Word* a Swedish morality play instead of catching Kaj Munk's spirit."

As Malberg later explained, when Molander made his version in 1943, Victor Sjöström played Morten Borgen. By that time, Sjöström had stopped directing films himself; he had often acted in his own works all along, most notably his role in *The Phantom Chariot* from 1920. Eventually, as he grew older, he worked only as an actor (in Ingmar Bergman's *Wild Strawberries*, among others), becoming Sweden's foremost interpreter of character parts. It had been no surprise to Malberg when Sjöström was given the role in that film.

Soon the table, which had been laden with thin slices of black bread and white bread, pilsner beer and milk, butter, fish, liver paste, chicken, ham, cheese, marmalade, and jam, was cleared to make way for heaping dishes of strawberries with cream, followed by coffee.

Malberg brought out a box of Havana cigars, presenting it to Dreyer, making a mock bow. "We are so happy to work with you, Herr Dreyer," he said, clasping his hand—no longer in jest but in real devotion—"that I had to make this little speech to let you know we have faith, no matter what the weather."

Out the window, a far hill became flooded with light at that moment. The company burst into cheerful cries, rose up from their seats, and pressed against the glass. The hill flickered, then went dark. Everybody rushed outside to look for signs of change.

Impatiently, we waited for the radio forecast, sent over the loudspeaker in the dining hall. "It will rain again tonight, in particular in the western parts of Jutland," Dreyer repeated when the radio was shut off. He lit a cigar for Malberg, testing his own. "Well, we must have more coffee, I beseech you," he told a waitress.

He smiled, turning to me. "There is something about coffee that soothes the Danes," he said, "and puts them in touch with God. We become philosophical about it. Coffee is the mainstay in Jutland in particular; the farmers like it with a little cognac. On Sundays they gather in each other's homes to discuss religion—sometimes to read poetry and plays.

"You will see they do not forget the teachings of Grundt-vig, who was the benefactor of the country folk. On the winter days, which last so long here in Jutland, a warm cup is a balm; they take everyday communion in it. Kaj Munk knew his people.

"The play *The Word* begins," he continued, "with a scene in which the family takes coffee. It is natural for them to sit with their coffee and troubles. That is perfect for the troubles. That is perfect for the stage, made to order. However, in a film you must *show*—instead of having the family talk about Johannes, I make the action direct.

"The family wakes up in the night; Johannes is missing, having gotten out of bed and gone through the door. His father, old Borgen, and his brothers, Mikkel and Anders, follow him over the dunes. On a hill in the moor Johannes gives a sermon to an imaginary crowd; his father and brothers strain their ears to listen. I think this is a natural beginning, too.

"I took up this change with Fru Munk; I have checked with her for everything, seeking approval. Because I want to be fair to Kaj Munk's intentions. The meaning must be unchanged—I must keep pure the flavor of the original, just as I, from the pages of Sheridan LeFanu, was inspired to make *Vampyr*."

The afternoon was gray and gloomy, yet Dreyer calmly went on. "You must revitalize a work when you give it a different form. You cannot merely try to copy. You must try to give it full value, shedding new light. Think of *Don Quixote*. Gustave Doré, Daumier, and Cruikshank all illustrated it, sticking to its heart but each time mining something fresh. Richard Strauss wrote one of his very best tone poems, and Pabst made a film with songs, having the idea to put Chaliapin in the name role. All these works were justified; none of them cheated Cervantes."

He puffed thoughtfully upon his cigar. "You know, Chaplin once was going to do a film on the life of Napoléon, with the Spanish singer Raquel Meller as Joséphine." He pronounced both names in the French manner.

"But he learned some big American company was about

to release the 'biography' by Abel Gance; he quit the project. Don't you think it would have been a wonderful chance for Chaplin? Instead of a Prometheus leading massed armies downhill, he would have shown the inner man."

His eyes rested briefly on the darkening sky. "So I am making *The Word* by feeling that it is my film but Munk's play. I am positive the two are compatible. Some people warn me against trying Munk's masterpiece. I must work hard to satisfy them. That means when you come down to it, I must do it as I see fit.

"This bad weather will pass. The last gate will open. Once these outdoor scenes are finished, we will not be hampered in the studio, though any delay here makes us suffer, since the contracts, every one, run only through the first of October. The Danish summer of 1952 was very rainy; we could not foresee this one would be as bad. Herr Malberg was telling me that in his youth in the 1890s there was a year like this—heavy and wet."

Henrik Malberg got up from his chair. "I'll go back to bed," he decided, "until there is more coffee. Or until the sun comes out. That is one way to beat dismal days. Anyhow, I have to rest up. Tonight I'm going to Vemb to see a film called *Adorable Creatures*. You come too, Herr Wahl." Next he shuffled out, puffing on the stub of his cigar. "Don't forget," he called back, "there is only one bath at the hotel."

Dreyer's assistant, Jesper Gottschalch, had found me a temporary room in the hotel. Gottschalch had to drive down to the seaport of Ringkøbing, since the ancient Dodge, which the producer Tage Nielsen had loaned for use during the making of *The Word*, had broken a spring and had to be fixed. When he returned, he would take me to Ulfborg so that I could check out of the inn there.

Dreyer walked me out to the driveway. In a few minutes he would return to the annex, where, in his room, he was about to meet Anne (Gerda Nielsen) and Anders (Cay Kristiansen) to discuss the love scenes. Both were young schoolteachers, and neither had acted in films before. He did not seem to consider their lack of experience a handicap.

I asked how it would turn out in the dialogue scenes for them. "It will be hard for all of us," Dreyer replied, "though not in the way that you might think. You see, no one has ever been able to make a sound film here in Jutland until now. The wind whips into the microphone, ruining the track. This is another obstacle to be passed. We must hope for success.

"Anne and Anders will grow into their scene, then we will wait for our chance. This is the kind of scene that Munk's theater structure cannot allow but is right for the film. We do not always use the same kind of scenes."

He explained: "For instance, I eliminated the story of Johannes's fiancée, called Agatha by Kaj Munk. Munk explains Johannes's madness partly by means of saying he collapsed after she was struck by a car while trying to save his life. The couple had just attended a play in which someone is brought to life by a miracle. Johannes, a theological student, while pondering the theme, steps into the path of the car.

"When Agatha lies in her coffin, Johannes is found trying to urge her up, imploring for a miracle. He faints and, upon coming to, assumes the identity of Jesus Christ. At the end, when Johannes is confronted with Mikkel's wife, Inger, who died in childbirth and is lying in her coffin, his mind returns to the moment when it was led astray.

"I simplified this for the sake of the film. Agatha was not necessary. You have to strip all things to their essentials. Johannes, according to the film, is a very enthusiastic theological student who has a nervous collapse. In clinical studies, such a case is very common. His concentration has developed to the point where he is under the delusion that he himself is the Lord Jesus.

"The young man Johannes, like everyone at the farm Borgensgaard, carries much love for Mikkel's wife and, believing he is the Christ, supposes himself to have the power of miracles; so with all his strength he tries to exercise this power. It fails; he does not possess the means and, in this second collapse, realizes he is not Jesus Christ.

"In both cases, the film and the play, the true miracle occurs after Johannes has regained his senses. Being then a sane man, not of impure mind, he has faith in the life-giving Word, as does Inger's little daughter. Together they ask God to release Inger from death; that is when the miracle comes.

"*The Word* can be made in only one manner: by believing. Kaj Munk uplifted not Vedersø alone but all of Denmark. So I want this film to carry his spirit around the world."

We stepped onto the hotel porch quickly to get shelter. And Dreyer continued, oblivious to the immediate wind and weather: "Kaj Munk described John the Baptist as being a man who was not extremely cautious, a man who spoke out the truth no matter the cost. In the end, the Spirit of God outweighs even Blood and Truth. Munk shouted accusations against the Germans, just as the Baptist had told the truth about King Herod.

"Well, after the New Year 1944, at last the Nazis took Munk away from his wife and five children; when we return to Copenhagen on the road to Ringkøbing toward Silkeborg, you will see where his murdered body was thrown in a ditch. A stone cross was erected there, and Danes lay fresh flowers at the spot every day.

"On the title page to *The Word,* Kaj Munk quoted something he heard from the widow of a Vedersø farmer. If we have faith like hers, he thought, we can believe it about her husband or anyone else. She said: 'Yes, his best clothes hang ready, for you really never know but what he may turn up one Easter morning.'"

All at once Dreyer asked: "Do you feel this part of Jutland in your bones yet? It's more primitive than Sealand out here. Look how poor the soil is. How the faces are burned in the wind. In the hall, before you turn in to the dining room, you can see a photograph hanging. It shows a Polish freighter that was washed ashore a year ago last winter. Whenever the iron bell clangs, each family here sends a man out on the sea—it means a boat is in trouble or has capsized. They have a system: each man is signed up for duty, and if he is away, he must have someone else responsible in his place.

"The rain's slacking; it may quit soon. Let's get set to move you into the hotel. They might even build a fire tonight. If you hurry, you'll be back in time for coffee."

He paused once again. "Now you can begin to understand how typical and perfect is the advertising slogan which you'll find in all the local newspapers. It has no equal, in fact, no meaning anywhere else in the world!" It claims, he told me with a wry smile:

NO SPIRITUAL LIFE
WITHOUT CIRKEL COFFEE

And he hurried into the annex to meet Cay and Gerda.

4   Lambs in the front yard

There was a tiny bluish, oval-shaped glass, a type of lens Dreyer usually wore about his neck on a cord, made for him by a famous Venetian glassblower. If you looked into it, you could anticipate how objects might appear on-screen, since color values were transmuted to tones of black and white and gray.

He'd gaze through it intently, standing in a field. Sometimes he assumed the role of a camera—squaring his hands in front, holding an invisible camera box. He would move forward as if rolling on a track, making a panorama of the landscape, gliding into it, then, just as rapidly, coming to a halt to focus and balance his composition.

He would remain a little apart from the remainder of the company. When he'd finally settled on the movement of his "camera," the equipment would be moved into place.

At seven in the morning we were at the farm that was to be Borgensgaard, owned by Valdemar Kristensen, a distant cousin of the Munks. The location was about a ten-minute ride from the Vedersø Klit Hotel. The enclosed buildings of the farm were directly beside the winding dirt road. A cobblestone court lay in the middle; the living part contained thirteen rooms and was two hundred years old. The pig pen, hen roost, and stable had been added on forty years previously, in about 1915.

Fru Kristensen, who was pregnant (as was Birgitte Federspiel, who was to play Inger), showed me the thirty newborn piglets. "Everybody has babies here," she laughed. "Our dog Polly is fat with child too. She's the lucky one; she gets to sleep under the oven.

"They took a picture of me already. I had to run across our field to get help for Inger, who was struck ill in the story. They took it three times, but I had to run twenty times in all because Dreyer wanted me to 'run nervously.'"

Next she told me she had to scurry back to the wash-tubs, but if I ever got bored, I should come inside; she had a copy of *The Poems of Robert Burns*.

It rained heavily at 6:00 A.M. The sky had been pitch-black. Now it was more blue-gray, yet the sun was not out yet. Some members of the company waited in the farm's drawing room; others huddled inside the van or the old Dodge. Among the latter was Henning Bendtsen, the bearded cameraman, as well as two apprentices, Erik Willumsen and John Carlsen.

I ran from the van to the Dodge to the drawing room,

wondering who wanted coffee: Jesper Gottschalch, Dreyer's assistant; Karen Petersen, the secretary or script girl; the makeup woman; and six crew members who handled sound, set up the camera tracks, or held the reflecting screens and such.

The shot we waited for was the one that opens *The Word*. Gottschalch was anxious. "The tone of this film has to be evolved in these early scenes. Herr Dreyer depends on the skill with which the technicians respond to his descriptions. It will be hard for him. Danish cameramen, even the best, are used to bad equipment, small budgets, always pressed for time, and in general not having the training to be able to carry out subtle effects. What Dreyer needs is sympathy—he won't always get it. He is too much of a perfectionist to suit them all. This isn't merely a job. This they must understand if they have intelligence. They must succumb to his personality; that's what it adds up to."

The name BORGENSGAARD in metal letters had been fastened to the house on the wall nearest the road. Gottschalch left to help two members of the crew, Herr Fuglsang ("Bird-song") and his son Bruno, try the silver reflecting screens on it. Clouds overhead were separating in slow motion.

Young Carlsen said, "This will be the greatest experience I have ever had. Every time *Vampyr* and *Day of Wrath* are shown I go to see them. Did you ever see such pictures? I want to learn a lot here. Look what we are given to use! Two old, old cameras. A silent one, a little German Arriflex model. And the big sound camera isn't in good shape either. Palladium bought it for one-fifth its original price from an

English company. But Dreyer knows how to bring out the best in them. My job is to handle the focus."

I was about to examine the camera closely. Carlsen stopped me. "Nobody is supposed to look through the lens except Herr Dreyer himself and Bendtsen. It's their private keyhole. Keep out of it. If you forget, you'll pay a fine—a drink for the whole technical staff!" Then he explained that Dreyer was to make *The Word* to fit the new wide screens. "He says he will make the normal size picture but will allow for enough head room for widescreen. There are lines marked off on the viewfinder for it."

To create the panoramic view of Borgensgaard, they were placing the camera in the field on the opposite side of the road, with a wall of sod and weeds built up to hide the roadway. Dreyer spent two hours composing the scene.

The clothesline, on the dunes next to the house, was hung with towels and sheets selected by him and arranged by Karen Petersen under his direction. Then Dreyer held a conference with Valdemar Kristensen's wife, Anne-Marie, who admitted she sometimes left clothes hanging out all night.

A half dozen lambs were coaxed to the front yard and tethered there. But Herr Kristensen raised an objection: on such a large farm, sheep would never graze so close to the house. Dreyer smiled and said, "I need a visual metaphor to start *The Word*. I will be *thematically* accurate."

A horse was tied to the fence, which would form the far left of the shot. The windows of the house were shut and barred. On the near side of the road, low in the picture, Dreyer added a plow and a wagon. He changed the positions of objects numerous times, pulling the wagon forward, then backward; trying the tongue of it up and then down; at last stripping the sideboards off, exposing only the skeleton of the wagon.

He shifted the lambs, alternating dark ones with light-wooled ones, next taking out half of them and using three alone. He removed the plow. "You live with it for awhile," he observed, "then you know what you need."

Because it was to be a night scene, a red filter was slipped over the lens. It was intended for the camera to pan gradually from the left (the horse in the field), swing across the yard to the right (the wall of the house), and come to rest upon the name BORGENSGAARD. Afterward, the camera would be set up for a close-up of the house, in case the letters were not distinct enough in the panning shot.

The sky was overcast again. Bendtsen tinkered with his camera. Dreyer kept scanning the heavens. Karen Petersen shook her watch. Someone who had been inside warming up came out the door, startling the lambs. They pawed nervously. Dreyer went over to them and spoke softly. In a few minutes they were calmed, nibbling grass peacefully.

Down the road on either side of the camera, both Bruno Fuglsang and Jesper Gottschalch were stationed to halt whatever traffic might come by during shooting. Suddenly, an abrupt shift in the wind revealed the sun. Like a tidal wave, yellow light rolled across the dunes.

Dreyer whispered, "In the tempo," and the camera whirred. The scene that day was filmed three times in succession, but it actually took several days to get the perfect shot he wished to use.

As things were readied for the close-up of the sign,

Dreyer said, "The wash on the line and the sheep grazing are there to give an impression of life. The dark sky and closed windows say clearly enough that it is night, but if shown alone, the feeling might be one of bleakness—perhaps of death. That would be wrong."

Soon we watched a canopy of clouds unfurl and halt the filming of any scenes to follow. Kaj Munk's widow and two of her children arrived in their car. It was after eleven; an indoor picnic lunch was served at Borgensgaard. During the winter months, Fru Munk lived in Copenhagen. In the summer, she lived at the parish house in Vedersø. Jokes and laughter and cigar smoke filled the dining room for hours. Everyone seemed in high spirits, having been honored by Fru Munk's presence. The coffee urn was brought in, mellowing the gaiety.

Fru Munk announced merrily: "*This* is the way I like to see a film; where I can sit in the chairs, walk through the doors, actually shake the people's hands!"

After two-thirty, Dreyer wanted to catch another shot, if the sun came out long enough. Henrik Malberg and Cay Kristiansen were brought in from Vedersø. The company, with Kaj Munk's widow leading, drove down the road until reaching a small valley. A wagon with a team of horses had been hired; the shot was to be of old Borgen and his son Anders racing home from Peter Tailor's house. Borgen had discovered that his son wished to marry Anne, but sour-faced Peter had refused. This insult crushed old Borgen's pride, so he went to have an angry quarrel with the tailor—who, in turn, prayed aloud for a miracle to humble the old fellow. Then the telephone jingled: at Borgensgaard, Inger had fallen deathly sick in childbirth. Before Borgen rushed off with his team, he gave Peter Tailor a box on the ear.

Inside the sound van, Fru Jensen, the makeup woman, trimmed Henrik Malberg's features. She removed his glasses, causing his eyes (slightly owlish and kindly) to become harder and penetrating. Next she glued on large bushy eyebrows. His whole face became imposing, more determined in character.

However, in the open air, Malberg was shy of the horses. Cautiously, Dreyer introduced them to him. Malberg and Kristiansen were boosted up into the wagon. They stiffened, gripping the edge of their seats. Dreyer showed Cay how to hold the reins; then slowly the young man let the horses trot down the road a mile or so. Malberg was sitting more boldly; finally, he took hold of the reins himself, clucking to the team until they galloped.

The wagon flew steadily along. Then Malberg jolted to a stop, waving his cap like a flag. Cay was allergic to the cold and wind and had developed huge black sores on his lower lip; he put a handkerchief to his mouth. "Will it spoil the picture?" he asked.

Dreyer replied that it wouldn't, because of the distance. It would not be noticed on the screen. "We must take you into Ulfborg for penicillin shots," he said. The young man refused to quit yet, so the horses were started up again, Cay protecting his lip as best he could.

Two fat red cows had been hired from a neighboring farm, one set on each slope. Borgen and Anders waited far behind the hill to the right, so they could make a running start.

Everyone was tense; minutes dragged. The thick clouds would not let the sun through. Fru Munk and her children left for home. The whole company, save for Dreyer, wanted to pack up as well and head for Vedersø Klit—to a fire, beer, and comfortable hotel chairs. They shivered in the wind, buttoning on their jackets. But Dreyer remained in his place, peering through the lens. The dull blanket spread overhead appeared solid. "You have to be stubborn," he declared.

The damp wind whistled. A large hole was ripped in the clouds, the light perfectly suited for the shot. Dreyer nodded to Bendtsen. Karen Petersen gave the signal, running over the hill. Old Borgen began racing the horses for dear life.

Alas, Henning Bendtsen had chosen that instant to swing the camera back and forth—"checking the picture"—and failed to catch them. They sailed past out of view. Bendtsen shook his head in agony.

The gap in the sky was immediately filled. A few drops of rain spilled out. It was after four o'clock. Dreyer announced the sun was not the kind he could use any later that afternoon. They would try another day; the company was dismissed. Henrik Malberg and Cay Kristiansen came racing up in a triumph. Malberg was told the bad news: the previous shot had been missed; the horses were no longer required. He wearily shrugged his shoulders and descended from the wagon. He fitted on his glasses carefully, then stripped off his false eyebrows.

"Wait!" he called out as the animals were led away by the farmer. "First let me tickle their ears!"

5   A feeling for atmosphere

Dreyer stood on a heath-covered dune facing the North Sea. "The sun was to set at eight twenty-six tonight," he said. The horizon over the vast water instead had an opaque glow, a ghostly haze brushed dimly with pink. From the southwest, a procession of black clouds was heading toward Vedersø.

"It is difficult, very difficult, Herr Wahl, for me to sleep these nights," he admitted. "I become so anxious—waiting for a morning with good light. We are caught in the middle of two low-pressure systems. If we had one strong rain, it might act as a stout broom and sweep the sky clean.

"You know, I was thinking of the old German idea of how to work. Joe May once told me in Berlin that he preferred to film an arrival of a train into a station by building the whole thing inside the studio. Then every breath was under his control. Of course, he was wrong; the atmosphere of the studio always betrays itself.

"I have faced many conditions. While making *Jeanne d'Arc*, the entire studio was torn down and a new one erected, so Falconetti and I had no roof, often, over our heads. The Rouen set was constructed solidly. Only a few interiors had to be finished in more detail to make them inhabitable."

And he went on: "The set for *Jeanne d'Arc* was no plaster illusion—it was real and continuous." He closed his eyes, seeing it clearly. "That is why I like Vedersø." And he opened them to survey the harsh landscape. "You are secluded but can have a feeling for the atmosphere. It was the same outside Lillehammer in Norway, where we made *The Parson's Widow*. Or in the part of Sealand called Hornbaek Plantage, which was ideal for the garden of Gethsemane in *Leaves from Satan's Book*."

His voice grew quiet. "A film must grow out of its material," he mused, "believably, naturally. That is why I do not care to use famous actors. With Greta Garbo, Marie Dressler, Conrad Veidt, or Mosjoukine, your eyes are drawn straight to them and nothing else matters. Dumas is just as good as Pirandello for their purpose.

"However, I once thought I could use Fritz Kortner. I saw him in the play *The Patriot*. He was much finer than Jannings for it—less fireworks, more real sensitivity. He stirred me greatly. I realized he was what I needed for *Mikaël*, which I was going to make for UFA. But Kortner was under contract for months ahead. *Mikaël* was a different milieu for me; it called for a kind of celebrity."

He paused. "Next, I hoped for Werner Krauss, who had been Caligari, but Erich Pommer the producer was then having a feud with Krauss and said no to my idea. Benjamin Christensen was in Berlin working at the same time I was; we got together and solved the problem—*he* would do the role!"

At nine o'clock, back at the hotel, Dreyer and I had coffee with young Gerda Nielsen, who was still wearing her Anne dress of plain blue cotton, and Sylvia Eckhausen, who was Kristine, the wife of Peter Tailor. Like Anna Svierkier, who had been Herlof's Marte in *Day of Wrath*, Fru Eckhausen was an actress from the provinces. Einar Federspiel, who was Peter Tailor, had appeared in the original stage production of *The Word* in the role of old Borgen. Federspiel's own daughter Birgitte, a professional actress, was to be Inger Borgen. Birgitte wasn't required for the outdoor shots; nor was Henry Skjaer, the Doctor. So they had not made the trip to Jutland. Inger's husband, Mikkel, was played by a popular actor from the New Theater in Copenhagen, Emil Hass Christensen. The Vicar was a young man named Ove Rud, who had played small parts at the Royal Theater, from which he borrowed his pastor's coat.

Soon all the other members of the cast came down for coffee, except for Henrik Malberg, who had already gone to sleep. Cay Kristiansen lived with his wife in a house down the road, in a loft that had been fixed with a bed and a coal lamp. Hass Christensen alternated with dialect coach Svend Poulsen, a student from the University of Copenhagen— sleeping one night in an attic of a private house at Vedersø and the next in a small bed in the annex behind the hotel.

The coffee hour was usually the only social event of the evening, except for the Saturday country dances at the hotel. I am a clumsy dancer, and when I tripped, everybody was amused, save a very concerned Herr Dreyer.

Most evenings, the work of the following day was discussed individually and planned. Scenes were gone over until they became familiar so that at the location site, they would take on new meaning—be attached to the surroundings and come to life. "The actors must feel it," Dreyer said with conviction. "That is the only way."

One time Dreyer turned to Gerda Nielsen. "Now Gerda, I have a story for you." Herr Dreyer refilled her cup. The vignette went like this: "When I was in Berlin in 1924 I saw Benjamin Christensen making a scene from a film with seventy people looking on. It was a love scene, and he was shouting through a megaphone, 'A little closer, now—grab her arm! Give her a kiss! Oh, *give her a KISS!*'" Gerda blushed deeply.

The next morning, rain was pouring down. Old Malberg had taken ill and kept to his bed until midday. Dreyer watched over him like a mother hen, convincing Malberg he must drink hot prune soup.

On the hotel's closed-in porch, Gerda Nielsen sat biting her finger. "I'm trying to raise courage to write my family," she told me. "I thought we were to be here two or three days at the longest. I am embarrassed to tell them always, 'Maybe I come home tomorrow.'"

July ended at last. One morning a letter from Ebba Dreyer arrived, and Dreyer read it to me. "I have not written before because of the rainy spell here at Rungsted," she reported. "In such blue weather it is hard to write." Herr Dreyer laid it in his lap and sighed. We certainly had blue weather.

Weeks passed with everybody standing by, rehearsing scenes, practicing camera movements. When a clear day was at hand, as many as eight different scenes would be shot; most were filmed three times each, with the company smoothly taking one accustomed setup after another. "These are old friends by now," Einar Federspiel remarked.

In the studio, Dreyer intended to film scenes in exact chronological order; however, out in the country, he took the easier shots first and then led up to more crucial scenes. He also made the shots as the light was best suited to them. He even attempted to direct the cloud formations. "My little joke," he said, with a rare twinkle in his eye.

We were accustomed to the ghostly sight of the wagon, bearing the coffin of Inger, crossing the landscape. It would emerge over and over from a rampart of dunes—then vanish in a twist of the road, its wheels creaking their leitmotif. It had small white wooden crosses sticking up. The horses were hidden under black blankets and hoods. The gnarled driver sat solemn and still as death itself; he wore a sad, tall silk hat and snapped an ebony whip.

"It isn't so quick as the one in René Clair's *Entr'acte*," Dreyer mused, "but Death has different speeds."

At the village of Madum, Dreyer found a church exterior he could use. The Vicar was supposed to walk through the gate into the graveyard, seen by Inger from her window. Ove Rud was a skilled actor and "could accept such suggestions,"

Dreyer said. Accordingly, he laid out a precise path for Ove to follow with tiny sticks and flat polished stones.

Jesper Gottschalch hired fifty geese (mostly white, exactly as Dreyer ordered) to fill up the lower portion of the picture. The goose girl was to guide them past, then curtsy to the Vicar. The birds kept squabbling and hissing until Dreyer calmed them. There came a torrential rain, and the company took shelter at the nearby schoolhouse and, under pictures of Hans Christian Andersen and the late King Christian IX and the Queen, ate *smørrebrød* with the schoolmaster.

A week later, the scene was shot twice between the hours of one and two. The goose girl was so proud of being in *The Word* that she insisted she be able to wear her shoes. Dreyer agreed. He tried the shot first with the whole flock of fifty geese, then took several away. "There is always the method of elimination," he reflected. The second time he tried it with the camera in a slightly shifted position. The Vicar walked up, and the goose girl came alone, carrying a basket of greens.

As she latched the small gate door and walked off, the gate suddenly creaked open. Somebody objected that it had spoiled the shot. Dreyer answered no, "because that's how it happened." And he added, "I think I shall prefer this one, since it is more simple."

The vestibule of the church, to be used in a later shot, was found at Hee. If the doors were opened, the light in the trees outside gave a nice contrast. This principle, found in certain Dutch interiors (such as paintings by Vermeer), Dreyer employed more than once.

At Borgensgaard, the camera was set up on trolley

tracks inside the cobblestone court. The shot was made in early morning because Dreyer wished the fields far to the east to be lit, creating, he explained, "through the arch, a kind of doorway or window into space." However, the inner walls were too much in shade, so he installed six lamps under the eaves. A plow was added beyond the road as a focal point, and chickens were shooed into the courtyard.

The scene was to have Peter Tailor, his wife, Kristine, and daughter Anne bringing a wreath for the dead Inger. The camera was to slide backward as they shuffled in. Dreyer decided Sylvia Eckhausen (playing Peter's wife) should hold a psalm book, so farm owner Valdemar Kristensen fetched one from the house.

Dreyer watched through the lens for a full twenty minutes or more. "Now it is fine," he declared, "but for one thing— she should carry a smaller book; this one is too heavy."

Karen Petersen ran inside Borgensgaard and returned with a black high school songbook. "Will this do?" she asked anxiously.

"Yes," he replied, and the shot was made.

That afternoon the film's producer, Herr Tage Nielsen, arrived from Palladium. I was shooed a distance away so as not to be witness to the brief discussion. Someone suggested its purpose was to give the director a scolding for delays—no matter the severity of the weather.

The producer's car was a slight improvement over the ancient Dodge. The brusque Herr Nielsen wore a shiny black suit and puffed away on a brown cigar much longer than Malberg's or Dreyer's. He was a character straight out of the pages of cartoonist Storm Petersen.

6 The rain and the fiddle

The lip of Cay Kristiansen had healed. And Henrik Malberg was well again. Scenes were to be shot of mad Johannes leaving the house at night at the start of *The Word*.

Preben Lerdorff's collar had to be turned up in a special way, as Christ's cloak, to frame his face; the coat was fixed in place by Fru Jensen with thread and needle. Sheep were to follow Johannes over the dune as he ducked under the clothesline. Then his father and brothers were to follow. Malberg was expected to stumble as he hurried up the hill. Cay was instructed for a full quarter of an hour in the manner of buttoning his jacket.

Red filter "night" shots demanded a bright sun. Dreyer explained, "Because *The Word* is a realistic film, shadows, tones, lighting all must give characters a rounded and plastic appearance. It could not be done in the style, for example, of Murnau's beautiful *Faust,* where the lighting had to originate from a single source in order to be allegorical, romantic."

Finally, the first important scene was to be attempted: the sermon of Johannes on the dunes. The day before, Lerdorff and Dreyer had already drawn into a kind of mental shell; in the evening, Dreyer took his coffee up to his room.

He told me the scene required "complete isolation of the actor." Only a skeleton crew would be on hand. Even Karen Petersen and Jesper Gottschalch were barred "so that Lerdorff can open up for the camera. He must not have the slightest distraction. He should feel no eyes are watching. Bendtsen and I must be regarded, at the most, as part of the apparatus. Then he can transmit directly."

Morning was announced with a thin volley of clouds. On the other side of the dunes, as Dreyer counted clouds, the hushed assembly waited near the sound truck. The gray covering thickened. Nothing was heard but the swell of the waves. Hours passed. The sun disappeared; then it rained. Reluctantly, Dreyer left for Borgensgaard, and Lerdorff returned to Vedersø Klit to rest.

I followed Herr Dreyer, a distant ghost. Minutes ticked away. I watched him light a cigar, pacing up and down, going in the door and out, often peering through his little blue lens or framing a picture with his hands. Through the quiet air (I was now sitting in the kitchen), rain pattered on the roof. When I spoke with him he said, "Time is our cross."

The following day the company tried again. The scene lasted three minutes; therefore, Gottschalch measured open spaces in the sky. "Blow the dirty clouds off to Sweden," Fru Petersen urged. The sound technicians grumbled, though they hoped Dreyer hadn't heard.

Hallelujah! A space in the sky suddenly appeared. It lengthened, freeing the sun. Bendtsen was able to take the scene twice. Immediately, the film was sealed in a can and put on the train at Ulfborg. In a shop there with Dreyer, we found a copy of Kaj Munk's autobiography for only eight kroner (about one dollar).

That afternoon, he and I took coffee with Fru Munk. She said Valdemar Kristensen had just informed her that he wanted to keep the name Borgensgaard for his farm, but he might have to get permission from the District Council, since in West Jutland there existed another Borgensgaard.

After we left Fru Munk, we took a tour across the heath. Briskly, Dreyer climbed a hill to look out and contemplate. Then he asked, "Do you recall the story of Saint Veronica? How she met Jesus on the way to Calvary and gave him her veil to wipe away the sweat from his brow? His features became imprinted on the cloth. Now I truly see for my Jesus-film the screen—yes—an immense Veronica's Handkerchief!"

The company returned from location in a rye field, where the love scene between Anne and Anders was practiced. Copenhagen was on the telephone with serious news.

Rushes from the important Johannes sermon had been developed—revealing a cut-off scrap of film lodged in the aperture of Bendtsen's machine. It caused a heavy scratch that tore straight down the image, rendering it useless. This meant that all the opening shots had to be done over. "The clouds must be matched."

More impediments occurred that week: power break-downs, camera jams, and sound out-of-kilter. At the rye field, wind crashed into the unprotected microphone held over the lovers' heads. Eventually, a hat was taped onto the boom to muffle the noise. The wind whistled through in any case. Dreyer's solution: shoot the scene with the silent Arriflex camera and dub the dialogue in at the studio.

On Saturday, the weekly country dance was held. An accordionist and a violinist played Danish folk tunes. Gerda arrived arm in arm with dialect coach Svend Poulsen. Willumsen, the camera assistant, entered the hall with brackish oil covering his skin. "I wanted to swim!" he blurted out. "The water was like ice. Not only that—I discovered some tanker has drained off this oil."

Fru Christoffersen, whose husband owned the hotel, came rushing in from the kitchen to warn him, "Don't you dare use *my* towels to wipe it!"

Einar Federspiel arrived with his wife. Early Sunday they would leave for Klampenborg to attend to his theater until he was required at the studio. His Vedersø scenes had been completed. "Ah, the words to this song are by Denmark's number one poet," he declared, cocking his ear.

"Adam Oehlenschlager?" I inquired.

"No, no, no!" replied Fru Federspiel. "He forgot—we have *two* number one poets!" They departed to enjoy pancakes with ice cream and strawberries and argue over who was Denmark's number one.

At the door, Dreyer paused to observe the dismal down-pour outside. "There is an answer to everything," he said quietly. "Perfectly simple. God is a little angry with me because I am not yet doing the Jesus-film."

7 Magic of the lens

A specialty of the hotel cook was fried eel. I grew fond of it and never would have guessed it was so tasty. Always there were several kinds of potatoes. The small Jutland potatoes are most delicious boiled and without skins, then sautéed with a light coating of sugar. The local bakery tempted us each afternoon with wondrous delights, flaky and devilishly tasty.

Since I was a student and had no work permit, I had no official capacity. However, I would fetch obscure objects required by Herr Dreyer—such as a 1925 Jutland newspaper. It had to be in pristine condition and from 1925, not 1927! I climbed on a borrowed bicycle to pedal up and down the road to dozens of farmhouses until I located a newspaper— which would only lie in a drawer on the set. But it must be the correct date, lest it break the spell of concentration, should an actor happen to see it.

It was exhilarating to speed through the brisk air, getting exercise after typing up so many notes or delivering hot coffee from Fru Kristensen's kitchen to whomever huddled inside the old Dodge and trying to calm anxious actors' frayed nerves. Local dogs seemed to sense I was a foreigner. They came flying at me, nipping at my heels.

It was a toothless widow in fastidious black garments who searched for and found the exact item I was seeking—a 1925 newspaper. Both of us rummaged through stacks of immaculately preserved newspapers—her entire life. I believed if I named any year in a hundred she might unearth it. And I brought the prize to Dreyer, who nodded, saying, "Excellent, Herr Wahl," as if he had not expected anything less.

Permission was granted for the company to drive with its heavy equipment onto the Husby Plantage. By law, ordinary visitors are admitted only on foot or by bicycle. Involved trolley shots were constructed; in one of them, Anne-Marie Kristensen and Cay Kristiansen were to be out searching for Johannes. The camera followed them on a long track. Anders (Cay) was to emerge from the bushes, go around a sheep shelter and search it, find it empty, then turn around and call the name of his missing brother—then dash out of the picture as the servant girl comes running down a scrub-covered dune from a different direction.

Soon a thick layer of clouds folded over, so Dreyer and the sound man spent an hour recording various people calling "Johannes! Johannes!"—the voices echoing throughout the *plantage*. A rather deep ravine among the dunes served as a natural echo chamber, and everybody was happy. Yet I sensed Cay was jittery. After all, this was his first significant solo moment, and he had rehearsed it time after time.

The sun returned; the camera was now in place and began rolling smoothly, smoothly along the track. Cay came out, explored the sheep shelter as he'd been instructed, cupped his hands, and shouted in earnest against the loud wind his own character's name: "Anders! Anders!"

No one said a word.

Immediately, Dreyer's eyes went absolutely blank. Sighing, he said, "We will dub in the correct name at the studio."

There were successes also. At Borgensgaard, the camera splendidly caught the return of Johannes, no longer insane, striding into the courtyard of the farm. It was a complicated shot, with Lerdorff in sharp focus in most of it. He was to pass under the shadow of the arch, departing from the camera, which halted momentarily and then turned its gaze upon the elderly driver sitting atop the hearse parked fifty feet distant. John Carlsen managed the trick with the quick shift of field superbly.

At Ulfborg, when the rushes were shown to a few of us, Dreyer raced up to Carlsen and clasped his hand. There were tears in his eyes.

Ordinarily, rye is cut down by the first week in August. The farmer who owned the field, which in reality lay ten kilometers away from Borgensgaard, let the rye lie fallow, as Dreyer wished. Early-morning or late-afternoon sun was demanded to give the "summer-diffused" effect the scene required. In it,

Anne sets out to deliver a pair of trousers for her father, Peter Tailor, but she takes the long way around in order to have a tryst with Anders. The lovers meet in the field, lingering at a corner in the rye.

The camera had a long traveling movement, its tracks laid on a wooden platform in the shape of an immense letter *L* whose angle was parallel to the field. On that day, between three and five o'clock there was sufficient light for five takes, allowing for shadows too variable or winds too strong.

While Dreyer went over the final nuances with Henning Bendtsen, the two lovers, as Herr Dreyer wanted, were not to be continuously centered on-screen: they were meant to hesitate, shyly drift apart, then touch and flee guiltily. These fragile moments had to be perfectly balanced.

Meanwhile, Gerda Nielsen was holding a cigarette but did not light it. She sat waiting in the old Dodge with Cay Kristiansen beside her.

Svend Poulsen sat in the sound van. I climbed in with him, and he spoke. "Dreyer is right. He claims Gerda by her nature will be just as Anne should be: sweet, timid, tremulous, like Lisbeth Movin [the young wife in *Day of Wrath*] was. I have gotten Gerda to speak with a touch of Jutlandic. She's a bit nervous. But once the scene starts, she'll forget everything except Anne—I mean be herself—in the situation. And the mechanical boxes disappear."

Dreyer kept studying the lens. Then Fuglsang pushed the camera along the track, and we climbed out of the van. "In the tempo," Dreyer was instructing. "That is better. Better!" The camera glided, halted, rushed forward, and lingered—

drew back and stopped. Finally, it slid and turned the corner. "The mood changes here," Dreyer indicated to Bendtsen, who stood with arms folded. "At the corner the light alters, the sun will be behind them. We want that."

He repeated the same pacing with Bendtsen and, when he was confident about the movements, told him, "Now we must forget about it a moment—we might disturb them." He indicated the two young people in the old Dodge.

Dreyer walked toward a dune beside the rye field to watch the sky like a sentinel, his left hand shading his eyes. He looked once again through the blue glass. Bendtsen and his wife (who had come along for the day) picked wild black-berries. The crew had brought tonic water and orange drinks and sat beside the road, shielded from the wind by the little gray truck.

A fresh new breeze rustled the yellow grain stalks. The camera stood fixed in position on the raised platform, idle, its lens uncovered. Cay Kristiansen got out of the Dodge and leaped over a ditch. He caught his foot in the thick grass and nearly stumbled. He crossed the corner of rye to stare at the awesome camera next to the wide field, the rising dunes, the road curving out of sight.

On impulse, he mounted the wooden platform and crouched behind the camera itself, shutting one eye, squint-ing through the forbidden lens. He remained there fully five minutes, never budging. The crew stood erect; Bendtsen, who should have been guarding the camera, was out of sight. Drey-er was immobile. Someone had peered through his camera.

The wind died down; we could no longer hear the sea.

The sky was clear. There was an awesome, terrible silence. Then Gottschalch shouted: "For God's sake, Cay! *Stand up!*"

The young man rose, as if shaken from a sleep. "Why didn't somebody say so?" Cay asked, descending and coming over toward the sound van. He weakly motioned with his arm. "I could have looked an hour through that lens. It made you want to crawl straight through it!"

8   Something about Jesus

The density of rain was not what plagued Dreyer most. The rainfall often was easy, though it never seemed to cease because it hovered over, threatening, even if the pattering stopped—ready to begin anew.

Some shots demanded full overhead or noon light; others demanded softer early-morning or late-afternoon sun. Technicians and actors were ready; the waiting was endless, a heavy burden.

Dreyer had already waited a decade to begin a new film. Now time was running out; Palladium expected the outdoor shots to be finished in a matter of days. Therefore, when the contracts had been drawn up in the spring, they covered only to October 1.

No one had foreseen such inclement weather. The exterior shots at the parish of Vedersø were expected to consume only a tenth of the film's total running time. Some crew members were scheduled to move on to other projects at Palladium or elsewhere. The young actors Gerda and Cay, both of them teachers, were obliged to return to their schools.

However, for Dreyer, these were not the main problems; eventually, there would be some way around them. Vedersø was to provide the milieu that must carry over to interiors at the studio. Dreyer's most vexing worry was that he was delaying the start of his chief and most cherished project, the long-planned Jesus-film. He had written the script in the late 1940s. *The Word* was a trial run for that project—a tantalizing sketch in preparation for the ultimate goal. But this film must stand on its own.

In the following days, whenever it clouded up or as we strolled together after an evening meal, he shared his vision. It wasn't enough to be making *this* film. Although this experience was important, the Jesus-film was to be his salvation. Until he was actually immersed in it, his soul would not be at rest, he confessed.

He must be given the chance to make *The Life of Jesus* (or *Jesus of Nazareth*) simply because he was capable of doing it. *The Word* was a thematic experiment for the Jesus-film. It was the grand beginning. Furthermore, Dreyer expected the Jesus-film to be in color. As he saw it, an artist proceeds from engraving to a wider field of color tones. Thus he would use widescreen or CinemaScope, if desired.

In both this current film and the Jesus one, there would be problems to solve, for he was dealing with an individual forced into a social group: Johannes in the midst of his family,

Jesus with the disciples. Because the context had expanded, longer dialogues were necessary. In his earlier sound films *Vampyr* and *Day of Wrath,* the dialogue was spare. Now Johannes must speak to his family and Jesus to the disciples.

Scenes composed of twenty to thirty or more joined cuttings, as was artful in the silent features, would spoil the unity. The camera here had to be held back; unbroken shots of five, six, seven, eight minutes' duration must be sustained. But how? The viewer could not remain stationary; that was not Dreyer's way. That would be theater. The solution was what Dreyer described as the floating close-up with a constantly subjective camera. This method particularly demanded precise camera work and rehearsing.

Dreyer carried out technical experiments during *The Word.* One day a shot was to be made just outside the fir forest, with the camera placed in a field with a far view of tall trees. And Johannes was returning home after his prayer at the *plantage.* His mind was now untroubled, his course clear.

On the other side of the path lay a grove of trees. Dreyer picked an open space with the forest in the distance. On the near side, he wanted a suggestion of trees. So we made a shadow of many leaves and branches created from a very long, narrow fishnet that seven of us held high in the air with poles or rakes borrowed from nearby farms.

Johannes was to step into the picture at the right, a greatcoat slung over his arm—the camera on a swivel as he strode out at the left. The shot had to be taken three times. It was an ordinary linking shot; however, Dreyer arranged it with his customary attention. He explained that he had never used a net shadow before.

In the Jesus-film, he intended to construct a wider canopy of long, thin strips like bamboo, with rings at the ends for support. He planned to attempt moving shadows with it, particularly if he wanted shadows across a face. There was an advantage to this: in certain biblical areas like Capernaum—now considerably more barren than they had been two thousand years ago—he could give the effect of vegetation where in reality it was lacking.

When we next sat together, he told me: "*The Life of Jesus* will be made in Palestine in the Hebrew language." However, he wrote the script in English to show the backers. "Nor will the film employ subtitles for world distribution. Instead, a narrator will be used to lead into the episodes. Yet once the familiar scenes begin, only Hebrew will be heard in order to give the feeling this is a document—not so much a 're-creation' as a record."

He continued, "Today's Israel is rich in talent for art, theater, music. I am not worried about finding the people I need. I will take Jews recruited on the spot and will import Italians to play Romans."

Whereas his Joan of Arc film did not demand music (not even the Bach with which it is sometimes accompanied), his Jesus-film would "have music that belongs to it—the ancient Hebrew." He had found certain tribes that retained chants and songs and instruments from two thousand years ago. And in a folk museum in Israel, there were phonograph discs made by music archaeologists. The writer Sholem Asch also put pertinent material at Dreyer's disposal.

"In this film," he went on, "Palestine is an occupied country under the yoke of a totalitarian regime, such as Denmark was during World War II—the people waiting for a Messiah who will free them. A collective psychosis makes them want him.

"Jesus—inspired by his cousin John the Baptist in the symbolic role of Elias, the herald, who was to prepare the Way, according to the Scriptures—assumed the mantle of the Son of Man foretold by the prophet Daniel. Jesus's death was a political murder ordered by the Romans. The form of his execution was not by stoning, which Jewish religious law prescribed at that time, but by crucifixion, purely a Roman means. The film will have also the object of combating anti-Semitism and the idea that Jesus was killed by the Jews."

Thirty-five years earlier, in *Leaves from Satan's Book*, Dreyer had treated Judas as a kind of Brutus figure, a tool of the high priest Caiphas, who was a direct ally to the Romans and to Pontius Pilate in particular. Herr Dreyer's basic view on the matter hadn't changed.

Also, he had already shown in another silent film, *The Stigmatized* (also known as *Love One Another*), made in Germany in 1921, Jewish people under the yoke of an oppressor. The story was laid in 1905 Russia, in a small town by the Djenpr whose citizens—half of them Jewish, half of them Russian—are consumed with, as he termed it, "eternally smouldering hate." The Jewish quarter is burned, and families are destroyed. A handful of fugitives flee to the border to what all Dreyer's people seek, and that is liberation.

His voice was full of emotion as he expressed his great sympathy for the Jews.

Dreyer intended *The Life of Jesus* to have no fade-outs or such devices. He declared that the film "will be continuous, one story leading directly into the next. Jesus will do and speak *only* what is written in the Gospel texts. But," he emphasized, "a number of problems arise, as anyone who has made the slightest comparison of the four Gospels is aware. They were handed down by means of the oral tradition of that epoch in precisely the same manner as the life and teachings of Socrates come to us from his pupils."

Here, Dreyer became so engrossed in the subject that he failed to light his cigar.

He continued, "We must ponder that a whole century passed before the word and deeds of Jesus got permanently recorded. Each Evangelist has his specialties. Among them, Mark predominates in dealing with miracles and exorcisms. John, whatever his discrepancies, gives invaluable detail to the last hours of Jesus's life. Little by little, many of the gaps are closed. And the four outlines taken together help build a combined portrait of what he said or did, although," Dreyer emphasized again, "they do not tell completely what he *was*.

"For that," he said, "we should hope to find the inner evidence—a stenographic kind of record that theologians designate as the missing fifth Gospel. For example: did Jesus really bear the Holy Rood himself to Golgotha? On the contrary, Matthew and Mark claim one Simon of Cyrene was forced to carry the cross, while Luke's version adds the brushstroke that Jesus walked in front while Simon, carrying the burden, followed."

I could not write it down fast enough.

"Our common picture of the scene is drawn from John alone—of Jesus metaphorically bent under the weight of the heavy cross. Fundamentally," he went on, "from those sources we have, we might conclude Matthew is the logician, the reporter of the discourses; Mark the historian, the reporter of the miracles; Luke the artist, the idealizer, the biographer; John the apologist, the reporter of the Passion."

Here, Dreyer was in command of the problems he must wrestle with. Our coffee was forgotten.

He summed up: "These glimpses can be fused only if the key is discovered. And if that is realized, the screen, illuminated, becomes a huge Veronica's Handkerchief representing the true image of Jesus the Christ!"

All the parables and miracles were to be included in the film. No matter the theory, the spiritual fact had to be shown. He added, "Jesus was a brilliant rabbi fulfilling a divine Messianic mission. Jesus the liberator antedated the philosophy of Gandhi in our own time."

9 In the end is my beginning

Dreyer's discourse invigorated both of us, and it was well past bedtime. He was sharing; I was absorbing. His main intention in *The Life of Jesus* would be to show with respect the Jesus that may have been, historically—not a figure devoid of breath, not an incantation hidden under gold and incense.

"Not a formula from Rheims or Augsburg," Dreyer stated, "but the Jesus of Galilee. To find him, it is essential to seek him out in his own place. To relive the Scriptures that he knew well, one must feel the suffering and humiliation." And Dreyer opened a drawer to bring out an English Bible; he read aloud in a half whisper from the book of Isaiah, chapter 53:

> Surely he hath borne our grief, and carried our sorrows: yet we did esteem him stricken, smitten of God, and afflicted.

But he was wounded for our transgressions, he was bruised for our iniquities: the chastisement of our peace was upon him, and with his stripes we are healed.

All we like sheep have gone astray; we have turned every one to his own way; and the Lord hath laid on him the iniquity of us all.

He was oppressed, and he was afflicted, yet he openeth not his mouth: he is brought as a lamb to the slaughter, and as a sheep before her shearers is dumb, so he openeth not his mouth.

He was taken from prison and from judgement: and who shall declare his generation? For he was cut off out of the land of the living: for the transgression of my people was he stricken.

And he made his grave with the wicked, and with the rich in his death: because he had done no violence, neither was any deceit in his mouth.

Yet it pleased the Lord to bruise him; he hath put him to grief: when thou shalt make his soul an offering for sin, he shall see his seed, he shall prolong his days, and the pleasure of the Lord shall prosper in his hand.

He shall see of the travail of his soul, and shall be satisfied: by his knowledge shall my righteous servant justify many; for he shall bear their inequities.

Therefore will I divide him a portion with the great, and he shall divide the spoil with the strong; because he hath poured out his soul unto death: and he was numbered with the transgressors; and

he bare the sin of many, and made intercession for
the transgressors.

Dreyer was revealing here the meaning of Jesus's sacrifice
and, consequently, how the view and the state of the world
become clarified.

"His last words from the cross are of importance. His
cry, 'My God, why hast thou forsaken me?' is the first line of
Psalm 22. It is significant because it describes the intensity of
his suffering. And through it he acknowledges the lesson he
makes of himself for others, his own sacrifice and fulfillment."

It mattered not that, at that moment, the rain was pelt-
ing down outside; we were in another world. Before bidding
me good night, he mentioned that the film would begin just
after the baptism of Jesus by John—at the point of the young
rabbi's entrance into public ministry.

"Where would *The Life of Jesus* close?" I asked.

Dreyer replied that he had three main choices: "after the
trial before Pilate, after the crucifixion, or after the resurrection." Recalling that John the Evangelist takes as his text
the book of Isaiah, he said, "I will end with the crucifixion,
at the point where the historical Jesus leaves us—such a film
must not only break ground; it must sanctify it."

In 1947, Dreyer happened to meet Blevins Davis of the
American National Theater and Academy (known as ANTA)
at Elsinore. When Dreyer informed him of his burning desire,
Davis's response was to offer a trip to America so that he
might work on the script. From then on, Dreyer felt totally
beholden to Davis, his personal savior.

Dreyer spent half a year at the Davis farm, called Glendale, in Independence, Missouri. When Harry Truman came to his hometown of Independence, the director and the president took early-morning walks together. Oh, to be an invisible bird over their heads, listening! What a joy that might have been.

Ever since that commitment to Davis, Dreyer was ready for the immense project. He constantly lived for it, awaiting its materialization. He spoke of preparatory work in Israel, where he worked out details of the film's style. He could commence at a moment's notice. Once the filming started, he intended to work straight through from beginning to end.

If need be, he planned an interim project: a study of Mary Stuart, beloved heroine of Schiller and Swinburne. He had done research in Scotland for it. Her motto "in the end is my beginning" might be Dreyer's own.

Keeping busy, he was hoping for the sign that he could move forward with *The Life of Jesus* after *The Word*'s release. Dreyer concluded, "I hope it turns out to be, as a sound film, what my *Jeanne d'Arc* was as a silent, only of greater dignity and beauty—the film of my life."

10 The word that crushes cliffs

The two or three days little Gerda Nielsen had envisioned stretched out for weeks. We drank lots of Fru Kristensen's strong coffee.

One morning during a downpour, "Vicar" Ove Rud and I took refuge in a shed at Borgensgaard. He mentioned the Stanislavsky method of directing, then turned to the Dreyer method. "He has in his head every exact movement or shade he wants," Ove told me. "The swing of the shoulders, the pauses. Everything is explained." So there was no need to refer to a script during the actual shooting.

We lightened the conversation when a flock of hens found shelter with us. I enjoyed the sight of Ove Rud in his Vicar's robe, surrounded, saint-like, by fluttering chickens. We amused ourselves by discussing the psychology of the birds that pecked near our boots, searching for invisible food. We decided they were pretty dim-witted.

The geese, however, were different. Somehow, Dreyer was able to enchant them by the power of his personality, perhaps connecting at an unknown level. He stared at them until he and the geese found a harmonious solution. During one shot, he wanted a black goose to wend its way in and out among white geese crossing the road. Ultimately, he was victorious.

Often, in the privacy of the hotel, Dreyer continued to explore biblical topics. To my relief, every now and then, out of nowhere, he shifted gears. Once, he mentioned that it was "impossible" to render an automobile satisfactorily in a painting. "But maybe the machinist Léger might try it!" he chuckled.

Obviously, Dreyer revered Henrik Malberg. The old fellow took more and more to his bed on chilly days. Dreyer admitted that he loved working with older actors "because they give themselves up to you more easily."

Often, on the location shoots, reporters and photographers intruded. Dreyer was always polite to them—winning them over by his lack of temperament, by his quiet demeanor, much as he had enchanted those geese. The sort of photo nonsense they wished for had little to do with the work at hand. One photo was of me, examining the clapper upon which Herr Gottschalch had written, as the journalists suggested: "ORDET, Scene I." It seemed to please them.

I took a tumble one afternoon while Gerda Nielsen practiced a scene; in fact, I fell three times into a low drainage ditch, lying there bleeding until Bendtsen's wife (who was again picking blackberries) improvised a bandage. That night I kept falling, even in my sleep.

By July's end, Ove Rud left for a vacation in Germany until he was required at the studio. Hass Christensen returned to Copenhagen. Dreyer insisted it was imperative to get perfect the key scene of the sermon by the mad Johannes. And he said he realized how he might improve the previous ruined scene.

Johannes had been too far back from the camera; therefore, Preben Lerdorff's expressions were not clear enough. So Dreyer set out with Bendtsen in the old Dodge, searching for a different spot for that scene.

The scene, to which I was not privy, was the crucial one in which Johannes's sanity totally returns during his "camping out" as he prays to God. The scene is notable, as well, because of the physical change that occurs in Johannes. Here, he abandons the appearance of the Christ. In shots directly preceding this one (though, in reality, shot afterward), Lerdorff isn't wearing a wig; it is his own hair parted in the center and combed straight to the sides. Since these shots are not in close-up, the difference cannot be detected.

I stayed in the sound truck as Lerdorff stood at the edge of a clearing in the evergreen forest. From a distance, I saw the crew holding the reflectors ready. In long shot, the picture is of Johannes, greatcoat over his arm, walking toward a pine tree. He sits. The close-up with dialogue lasts two minutes.

In earnest, he prays: "Jesus Christ. It pains me to see my brother like this, here where two people really loved one another and then Death broke the cord between them. Tell me, Jesus Christ, if it is possible to give her a return to life.

"Hear it—give me the courage, power, and the faith. Give me so strong a faith that I in your name can conquer Death. Give me the Word, the Word that is like fire, the Word that crushes cliffs—the Word that breaks the seal of Death."

He pauses. "And give me a sign so that I know you have heard my prayer."

Dreyer wrote the speech out for me that evening.

During this speech, Johannes runs both hands through his windblown yet still center-parted hair to brush it back, becoming the "old" Johannes. After this prayer, he closes his eyes. Then there is a blinding light—made by maneuvering the gold and silver screens to reflect on his face. The sun emerges from the clouds; he accepts this as proof and says, "The sign. The sign!"

That night, Dreyer heaved a great sigh. A director must always be prepared to remake a shot, be ready to do it a new way. A painter, he declared, has a big advantage: "He can make many sketches before he does the final painting. A filmmaker must use his only tool, the film itself, in order to *see* his image." He added that he was not letting Lerdorff or any of the other actors watch the rushes.

He admitted there were complexities a cameraman could not handle. Bendtsen sometimes failed with the shot; the sky would blacken too much and Bendtsen would give too sharp a black-and-white contrast, whereas Dreyer wanted a much softer tone. A member of the crew once remarked, "Well, Bendtsen often is not 'in tune.'" I observed that Bendtsen was sometimes loath to give in to the master and would stalk away. Dreyer would take coffee in his own quarters until the rift got settled.

Usually it was John Carlsen, the assistant, who was more in tune with Dreyer's wishes. Carlsen's loyalty to him was evident and touching. Some crew members grumbled privately that Dreyer was "old stuff," although years later, Bendtsen claimed that working on *The Word* was the finest experience of his life. So Dreyer had to reckon not just with the elements but also with his crew.

On another occasion, Herr Dreyer spoke on the subject of lighting in the studio. For instance, in his 1922 film *Once upon a Time,* Clara Pontoppidan, as the Princess, was lit up from behind to create a halo effect in her hair. This was accomplished with a Jupiter lamp—a lamp with a bare, un-protected coil. It proved so strong that whenever it was used, Pontoppidan became blinded and had to be led home. In or-der to learn what she had suffered, Dreyer stared straight into the Jupiter lamp until his vision was obscured with yellow spots for the next twenty-four hours.

Dreyer was eager for the controlled conditions at Pal-ladium compared to the vagaries of the climate in Jutland. "Rain, rain!" he said wistfully. "In 1890-something there was a rainy July—but this summer is history in the making."

Now it was August. The weather continued to be unco-operative. Gottschalch revealed he had a sinking feeling and sensed he had to approach Dreyer with caution. He wished to help but could not figure out how. He concluded, "No one can deny: Herr Dreyer is a man standing alone."

If a shot turned out to be satisfactory, Dreyer became

relaxed. And everybody relaxed. He almost always managed to give an impression that he was calm, no matter what, during this period of travail. As mentioned earlier, when he got upset, his eyes went eerily blank.

On a moonlit night we strolled along the dunes, not talking. Dreyer was deep in reverie, yet he gave an impression of being in good cheer because the scene that day had gone well. Even a nasty wind had failed to ruin the take.

On a high dune he stopped. He announced that in several days he would permit Bendtsen—since only two shots without actors remained—to make them without him. Besides, it ought to boost Bendtsen's ego. In the upcoming studio scenes, the cameraman might be more in sympathy with the director.

Back at the hotel, Dreyer asked if I cared to add a note to his wife at the close of a reply he had written. Curiously, he had written in pencil. Ebba Dreyer suggested that when they were back in town, I would be welcome to stay with them. I knew this would be an intrusion at a crucial time, with the indoor scenes beginning. Reluctantly, I declined.

Next morning, the newspaper *Politiken* revealed to us that Italy, Germany, France, Spain, and England all had glorious weather over the past three weeks. Somehow, Dreyer did not find it humorous. The afternoon Dreyer and I departed, Vedersø suffered a genuine wallop of a storm.

11 Leaves from a journal

Herr Dreyer sent a car from Palladium Studios to pick me up, after our return to Copenhagen. The interior sets were being finished at Hellerup, so he begged me to "taste them." He was immensely pleased with the work of Erik Aaes, the designer.

As I was taken through the constructed rooms of the farmhouse, Borgensgaard, I marveled at the painstaking, Dreyeresque realism. Each room was connected to the next exactly as it would have been in the home. The following pages are directly from my journal.

14 August, Saturday. Bendtsen was left to finish two shots: the one at the church at Hee, which D. says didn't have enough light, but the darkness can be softened by a chemical process in the laboratory.

Also shot of village with flags at half-mast. D. says this turned out excellently.

At Palladium a young girl of about 7—was greeted very affectionately—and her mother had a meeting about the role of Inger's older daughter Maren. She is from Ødense.

Afterward, D. took me through the interior of Borgensgaard—also Peter Tailor's—the latter not quite completed.

I spent the afternoon with Erik Aaes, who built the sets for *Day of Wrath,* which he said was shot in five months. Thinks *The Word* can be finished by October 1st. Shooting scheduled for Tuesday.

Backdrops for all of courtyard can be viewed from the kitchen or living room. The dunes and sea, viewed from bedrooms and living room, painted in tones of gray.

The near outside walls have imitation brick construction of plaster, as do all exterior walls.

The sets built in five weeks—with four carpenters and four painters.

Seven rooms have been built for Borgensgaard. Of course, the construction is a whole; however, most of the walls are what is called "floating." That is, can be set back or raised to ceiling of the stage to make room for camera.

There are two sound stages at Palladium filled by these two sets, Borgensgaard occupying the latter.

Borgensgaard has an outer kitchen—A, where slaughtering, washing, and bread baking are done. Tile floor. Dull white molded walls.

The kitchen itself, *B*, has board floor, yellow walls, big black iron stove, long wooden cupboard along the courtyard side, with three windows.

The living room, *C*, follows next, and as D. remarked, this is oversize. However, camera will never catch entire space.

Three walls are gray, but fourth—looking out to sea—is brown Dutch tiles (clever painted glazed reproduction). A large photograph of Grundtvig. Telephone book from 1924 Jutland. Board floor, six rafters on "ceiling."

Of course there is no ceiling.

Old Borgen's bedroom, *D*, has gray board floor; a framed small tapestry picture of Jesus above the heavy bed. Three rafters.

E: the bedroom of Anders and Johannes, beds placed head to foot along the window wall. Gray board floor. Altar book and a hymnal on the shelf above J.'s head. A photograph of a Grundtvig schoolroom. Small colored picture of Christ crucified.

F is the bedroom of Inger and her husband Mikkel. Again, gray walls and floor, but trimming and furniture in a gray-white. Twin beds, etching called "Aurora" hung between. Incidentally, all clocks are wound and going, although the actors, cameramen, etc. are not in town yet.

There is a child's bed also in this room, and a doll's bed beside it. Old Borgen's room has an ancient small hobbyhorse.

G is not completely furnished; anyhow, the large entrance hall leading to it is newly varnished and cannot be walked through. *G* is room used by special celebrations, weddings, and funerals. This is where Inger will lie in her coffin. Gray walls and floor, though the entrance hall has gray *papered* wall and brown wood floor.

By the way—a child's picture book lying on a ledge in the living room is dated 1929. Inger's knitting is in several places.

The painted drops seen from windows reproduce exactly the barn and courtyard at Borgensgaard and were executed by one man who often works with the architect on theater sets.

Three of the cupboards in the kitchen are real cupboards that open. As the architect told me, it was not the idea to make the place seem a museum but a lived-in contemporary home.

The backdrops are gray, "but not too dark."

There are still boxes of plates to be unpacked, more flowers in pots, etc. Camera tracks (none have been put in place) stacked up.

Earlier in the day a different girl and her parents had come out to talk with D. I was then alone in the sets. The lights were put on all day for me. However, he told me this afternoon he decided on the other girl.

Svend Poulsen arrived to spend late afternoon with the chosen girl and with D., working on her speech.

Wandering and sitting among the sets, I remember how D. always knows the angle he wants, things placed, the height for the pictures (which have no glass—not to reflect light), how many, many old books arrive and D. goes through each carefully, taking out what he thinks proper.

Always stripping things down to make an effect simple.

"Never be afraid to make things too bare," he says.

When he puts a cooking spoon (wooden) in a spoon rack he decides upon three—not four (which he placed at first); dark-colored spoon just so, the big one so. Choosing the items for the cupboards. Putting a thermometer at the window in front of Borgen's favorite chair.

A carpenter nailing things up in the kitchen pointed to a large blank space on one of the yellow walls—asking, "Don't you want something—to fill that up?"

"No," answered D. "Lerdorff plays a scene against that wall."

If D. moves objects or takes them out of sight, his practice is not to hesitate—because he knows the effect he must have. D.'s most-used expression with actors or carpenters: "That is better."

15 August, Sunday. Spent the day with D., wife Ebba, son Erik, and daughter Gunni. Their flat has large photographs of Indian temple sculpture. Good food, subdued talk, nothing about film—a subject verboten.

16 August, Monday. Preparations for lighting. At least twenty floor lamps. Some dozen hanging spotlights being suspended high above the walls of Borgensgaard's living room.

There is a nearly circular camera track now arranged on floor.

Today I have permission to go into the mourning room: windows with long, white curtains. At one end of room a fine black stove; at the other, two fake doors—the *death doors.*

Erik Aaes tells me that sets to *Day of Wrath* were done solely in tones of gray, with the exception of most pieces of furniture, which were brown wood. At lunch—which I had privately with D.—he considered it "tones of white."

D. tells me a letter has arrived—saying Louis de Rochemont might be interested in the Jesus-film—perhaps through Allied Artists! So Blevins Davis writes.

D. elated.

The shot on the circular track is just after the first ones—the one of a panoramic view of Borgensgaard and next one showing Anders in bedroom, awakening—finding Johannes gone—then that outside shot of Johannes walking away out of sight over the dune.

And—this involved shot, which will be from the living room as described.

Bendtsen and all technicians on hand. Also Birgitte Federspiel, Malberg, Hass Christensen, Cay Kristiansen—so tests can be made and the shot attempted.

Anders comes out of his room—steps over to old Borgen's room to awaken his father—crosses the living room, and goes out into entrance hall (the wax is now dry) while the door from Mikkel's and Inger's room opens. Inger also appears.

Much discussion. Timing of movements. How quickly should Cay go? At what point exactly does Birgitte open the door?

They grow a bit flustered and depart.

I roam around.

A new-baked loaf of bread is now on the kitchen cupboard.

source. She was honest and naïve. She must be treated
in that way. Now, Ingrid Bergman *(is a very fine woman and)* has much talent, however she was not right for the role——just as she was
not right in For Whom the Bell Tolls——because, no matter
what you say, Bergman is too ~~modern and sophisticated to~~ *much a product of modern*
culture and civilization to
portray a *(premative)* peasant girl."

We ate the last of the whipped-cream pastries. Before
Mrs. Dreyer took the tea-tray inside, she said, "During
the war, Falconetti, Louis Jouvet and others went to
South America to perform. She soon fell upon hard times. *Living bad*
opening a drama school to make her
She ended up in ~~a small town, taking in~~ *the* a few pupils."

"Falconetti died there," her husband said. "She was
our friend."

It was almost the hour for my train. Dreyer telephoned
the station, checking its arrival-time. "I shall be
leaving for Vedersø in two weeks," he said. "The interiors
will be completed in the Copenhagen studios by then, so
that when we finish with the outdoor scenes in Jutland
there will be no delay. We'll go directly into the interiors.

"In May, Mrs. Kaj Munk ~~and Jesper Gottschaloh, my assis-~~
~~tant,~~ went with me to Jutland, helping find 'motifs.' We
would choose two or three sites for each, talking over
their points every night until midnight. All the platforms

17

Coaching the little sister (deleted scene): Susanne Rud
and Dreyer.

Dreyer looks through the camera, with Karen Petersen (script girl) in the background.

Dorothy Lovell's pencil
portrait of Dreyer, 1954.

Identity photo of Jan
Wahl, Copenhagen, 1954.

Valdemar Kristensen (owner of the farm), Erik Aaes (set
designer), Dreyer.

Gerda Nielsen and Dreyer get acquainted.

(*Above*) Lunch break (left to right): Dreyer, Emil Hass Christensen, Henrik Malberg, Karen Petersen, Jan Wahl (in black sweater), Cay Kristiansen, crew members. (*Below*) Kaj Munk's widow comes to visit (left to right): her daughter, Dreyer, Emil Hass Christensen, Fru Munk, her son.

(*Above*) Setting up a shot on the dunes (left to right): Jesper Gottschalch (Dreyer's assistant), Dreyer, John Carlsen, Erik Willumsen. (*Below*) A child looks through the camera as Preben Lerdorff, Henning Bendtsen, Dreyer, an unknown man, and John Carlsen look on, while Erik Willumsen sets up a shot.

Waiting for the sign: Johannes (Preben Lerdorff).

Looking for Johannes: his brother Mikkel (Emil
Hass Christensen), his father Morten Borgen (Henrik
Malberg), and his brother Anders (Cay Kristiansen).

Cay Kristiansen, Henrik Malberg, Birgitte Federspiel (Inger),
Hass Christensen.

Anne (Gerda Nielsen) takes leave of her father, Peter (Einar Federspiel).

A shot maybe too beautiful to include.

(*Above*) Meeting of the "sour-faced" ones. (*Below*) Coffee and lovers: Cay Kristiansen, Sylvia Eckhausen (Anne's mother), Gerda Nielsen.

"Come over to our side": Henrik Malberg and Einar Federspiel.

Cay Kristiansen, Henrik Malberg, Einar Federspiel, Gerda
Nielsen, Sylvia Eckhausen.

Blessed are the children: Preben Lerdorff and
Elisabeth Groth (the older sister).

Waiting for the news: Emil Hass Christensen, Henrik Malberg, Cay Kristiansen.

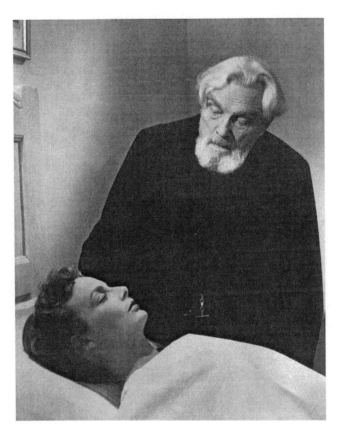

The birth room: Birgitte Federspiel and Henrik
Malberg.

The funeral scene: Cay Kristiansen, Birgitte Federspiel, Henrik
Malberg.

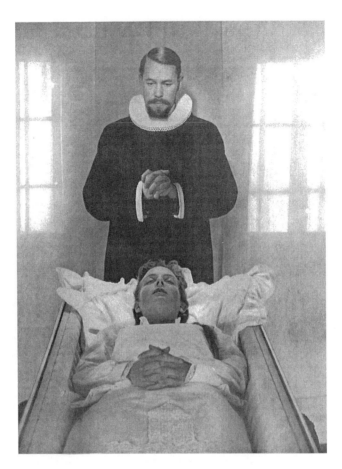

The Vicar (Ove Rud) prays over Inger (Birgitte Federspiel).

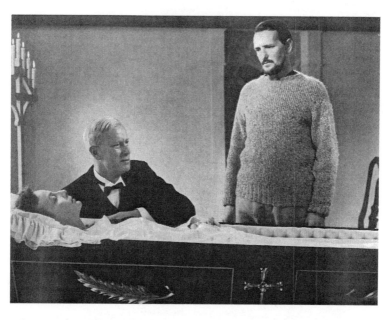

Johannes now clear of mind: Birgitte Federspiel, Emil Hass
Christensen, Preben Lerdorff.

A child can believe: Preben Lerdorff and Elisabeth Groth.

Now the life begins: Cay Kristiansen resets the clock.

Jokingly, I tell Karen Petersen about the 1929 child's book; she says yes, D. is aware of it, but unless a more correct book can be located, he likes the *cover* on that one. . . .

Besides—she has spent most of a hectic day searching for a 1924 Jutland newspaper. (What happened to 1925 newspaper I delivered?)

The woman from the studio's canteen is placing silverware in the chest of the living room during a lull—strictly under the supervision of D. and Aaes the architect.

D. also checking on prop books again—and pulling down the blinds of windows in the room of Johannes and Anders.

D. decides Anders would own a camera—lays well-worn black box camera at the boy's windowsill.

He rearranges the altar book and tablet and pencil at Johannes's sill. This is one reason he'd never go to Hollywood. "If I move a flower pot, I must go to the florists' union!"

He notices the tapestry picture of Christ above old Borgen's bed has a "good likeness to Lerdorff."

That pleases him.

At the desk in the living room sit samples of seeds and, at the window above, a rack of test tubes with seedlings. "A progressive farm!" he chuckles.

The pair of doors in the festival room, as noted, lead nowhere. They are mounted "on fearsome feet."

There will be a clock on the wall, stopped—which Mikkel sets into motion at the film's end when Inger sits up in the coffin. One cupboard. Otherwise, the room is quite bare, stripped of any festive air.

It's amazing how lighting brings a set to life: now arranging lamps outside the windows, Ove Hansen and other men are giving an effect of early-morning light—more correctly, "moonlight."

Earlier, D. and others made the beds—plumping them, making them look "slept in."

Rather chilly here in the studio, so Cay Kristiansen and Henrik Malberg remain fully dressed. Birgitte Federspiel has blanket wrapped about her.

D. rehearses Anders awakening his father. Malberg, lying in bed, wears nightshirt. Studio workers cleaning windows, brush the glass—Herr Stohl pushes out a whole window! While crash is considerable, D. so engrossed at work with Malberg he hasn't noticed.

Window being silently repaired.

Part of the microphone boom just fell on Malberg's head; however, he takes it in good humor.

Inger (Birgitte Federspiel) in nightgown, robe, with manuscript, comes now marching through the set. D. takes her into the bedroom and talks to her. Hass Christensen wandering about in stocking feet.

This Borgensgaard is from 1822; a line from Scriptures dated and hanging on the entrance into the hall:

GOD IS WATCHING OVER YOUR
ENTRANCE AND EXIT FROM NOW
UNTIL ETERNITY. AMEN.

Birgitte Federspiel is pregnant, exactly as Inger is supposed to be.

All the players' shoes soled in red felt. D., Bendtsen, and the technicians wear sneakers.

3:40: Still working on lighting effects. Malberg falls asleep in his bed; despite the hubbub, he snores.

"Working with people in bed again," D. says, "I am reminded of *Vampyr*!"

D. in another world—walks about imagining he is a camera; has his hands in front of him chest high, as if holding the lens.

B. Federspiel lies comfortably in bed after having her hair tied in long braid down her back.

D. busy hanging three tennis balls in net on one of the hooks in entrance hall. Johannes is a tennis player?

D. arranges coats and hats in the hall, then orders hobbyhorse taken from the old man's room. This awakens Malberg—who pops out of bed, putting on pants—and shoes—runs up to the canteen for a pot of coffee.

Again D. practices with Birgitte how Inger must open her door looking out—*Dreyer as Inger*. He glances right, next left—out the window. They do this over and over. And over.

4:45: All actors dismissed.

D. rehearses with Bendtsen, Carlsen, and Willumsen the camera movement from the entire scene. D. speaks with Cay (Anders), who remained behind, worrying about how he comes out the door.

Crew were promised they can leave at five o'clock, thus at 5:00 sharp, everybody scuttles away.

On the journey back to Frederiksberg, I ask D. how will he recognize his Jesus for the Jesus-film.

His reply: "Simple. I will recognize him when I am face-to-face with him."

12 Did they catch the ferry?

Ebba Dreyer cooked a terrific meal the next Sunday before I left Denmark. Goose, actually. I hope not from Vedersø. Herr Dreyer made it clear that for all studio scenes he must work in isolation, and I recognized it was prudent for me to accept the scholarship at the University of Michigan. I was loath to take leave of the Dreyers—the end to the evening was poignant. I describe the finale in my book *Through a Lens Darkly.*

I returned to Copenhagen by bus and by ferryboat. The latter crossing reminded me of the short film by Dreyer I admire the most. Therefore, Ebbe Neergaard of Statens Filmcentral arranged for me to watch it once more before I left the country.

In 1948, it was proposed that Dreyer direct a one-reel film concerning road safety. *They Caught the Ferry* is only twelve minutes in length, an impressive, eye-catching spine tingler. His sponsors were given more than they bargained for. He took the idea from a story by the Danish Nobel Prize winner Johannes V. Jensen. *They Caught the Ferry* doesn't require music, and it gives an impression of one breathless fatal ride.

A ferryboat is seen—a motorcyclist and his girlfriend depart. The man inquires as to when the next ferry on the other side of the island will leave; he's informed that he can't make it, there's not enough time. Nevertheless, he is determined and speeds off, the lady clinging on for dear life.

Dreyer's camera races with him, sometimes lagging behind. The motorcyclist takes chances, darting in and out of traffic—on the open road he is possessed—leaning forward on the handlebars, every muscle strained. He whizzes heedlessly along toward destiny.

It is necessary to stop for gas. He checks his watch. They may make it after all. So the motorcycle hurries away, his passenger begging him to take care.

She is frightened—clasping him tighter and tighter. He goes faster. An odd-shaped speeding vehicle looms up ahead out of nowhere, blocking the horizon. If the motorcyclist swerves to the left to pass, the other vehicle deliberately does also. If he swerves to the right, it does the same. At last, the motorcyclist catches up: they are neck and neck. The man turns to glance beside him—a hearse, painted white, with Death itself steering.

The motorcycle flies off the road—a crash. They catch the ferry.

A muffled drumbeat: Charon carries two plain white coffins across the water.

Jeanne Heimburger, a beautiful woman I knew from the Educational Foundation, my connection while I was studying in Denmark, told me, after she viewed *They Caught the Ferry*, "I couldn't touch my car for a week. When I finally did, I drove just twenty miles an hour."

In this black-and-white short, Dreyer creates a milieu to pull you in. And you can't escape: this is Dreyer in a nutshell. If, by the close of *The Word,* he wants you to believe in miracles, you will. You can't help it.

Dreyer first viewed D. W. Griffith's *Intolerance* as a young man in 1916. To this day, it remains a staggering display of massive architecture, tremendous crowds (all real—no digital fakery or Schüfftan process), a huge creation crying out against Tyranny and Injustice—an experiment employing new devices of cutting, framing, angles, inventing techniques as needed. According to Dreyer's own words, "I went home completely dazed, overwhelmed by a new rhythm and the number of close-ups. In particular those of Lillian Gish at the conclusion."

On that night, Dreyer became aware of how far one might aim in the medium. His method, ever since, was rooted in the possibility to isolate, narrow down, penetrate into, pierce, and magnify. It became not only the means but also the philosophy. Burrowing his way straight inside, he cuts through layer after layer until he consigns the individual to soul and to God.

"We are alone," was his credo. "We exist and suffer alone. We can only know, to our fullest extent, what we *feel*. Most important is the triumph of the soul—incorruption against evil, cant, lies."

As I packed my bag, I carefully laid my notes and journals on top of my clothes as the most precious mementos of my stay in Denmark.

I returned to America on a venerable Norwegian liner, the sturdy *Stavangerfjord,* a rough, storm-tossed crossing of eleven days. Jutland's awful weather accompanied me most of the way home.

Afterword

I received a fascinating postcard from Herr Dreyer once, yet to my regret, I managed to lose it. It stated that while searching out locations for *The Life of Jesus,* he had planted a tree in Israel in my name. I was deeply moved by this gesture.

I recalled an evening at the Dreyer flat on Dalgas Boulevard in Frederiksberg when he revealed a possible theory as to the character of Jesus. He suggested that Jesus was an insane (too strong a word, perhaps), brilliant young rabbi, truly believing himself to be the Messiah.

Dreyer stared at a blank spot on the wall and fell silent. I didn't press the matter further. The Jesus-film never did get under way, although the script has been published—a model of economy, a beautiful script.

Herr Dreyer and I kept in correspondence. I wrote children's books, but meanwhile, I worked on my Dreyer project and he would correct and edit, chastising me gently. Ultimately, I put it in a drawer until I knew I had to share that summer. I hope I have even in a cursory fashion sketched how a great film poet works.

In 1966 Dreyer came to New York's Lincoln Center for the American premiere of *Gertrud*. It was to be his final burst of energy. The audience was respectful of, if puzzled by, this slow-moving, innovative film. The theme of *Gertrud* is nothing less than love itself—a woman demanding total fulfillment of it.

When Nina Pens Rode, as Gertrud, sits on a chair or sofa to discuss with a visitor lost love or half love and they talk and talk and talk, some viewers groan audibly. Dreyer pares down his action, until visually, sometimes what catches the eye is a lone shifting, flickering shadow. And he does not employ close-up or much moving camera to aid the viewer. Unlike in *The Passion of Joan of Arc,* the camera keeps an objective distance.

The Danish government ultimately awarded him token monies (the sum of 300,000 kroner) toward the goal of which he was dreaming: the Jesus-film. It came too late.

At Lincoln Center, Dreyer was frail, very hard of hearing, too worn thin from futile efforts over many, many years. On a personal level, I realized I was no longer Herr Wahl, his dinner companion at the hotel in Vedersø with whom he had shared sincere hopes for *Porgy* (from the 1925 novel by Dubose Heyward, not the opera by George Gershwin), for *Mary Stuart*, for *Medea*, for a Technicolor Viking extravaganza that might, he hoped, sweep the world triumphantly.

I held his hand for a brief instant.

The pulse was feeble; his light-blue eyes were clouded over with visions that only he could be aware of. Then he turned away.

"Now the life will begin"

Dreyer's introduction
for actors in the film

It is important in the film based on the play *The Word* that the minds of the audience right from the beginning are made receptive to the great miracle: the awakening of Inger out of the sleep. The abrupt switch-over from the natural to the supernatural must be prepared in a much more careful way in the film than in the play. This can only be done by letting the audience get acquainted with the family in Borgensgaard—before the actual plot starts, that is to say, the plot of the play—so that the audience knows the attitude of each member of the family toward the others and how each person looks at the central problem in the play: Christianity and Faith. The film must also right from the beginning give the audience an idea of the psychic burden under which the family in Borgensgaard lives because one of the sons at the farm, Johannes, is mentally sick.

To fulfill this purpose I found it necessary to construct an opening which by and large is my own work, but I hope people will find that it harmonizes with the atmosphere in Kaj Munk's play. Apart from this beginning I have closely followed Kaj Munk, but I have tried to simplify the dialogue, as it should be remembered that the film according to its form—contrary to the stage—demands that speech from the screen to the audience must be simple and easily understood so that it can be grasped at once and without speculation. I have also worked on the assumption that Kaj Munk himself would have preferred a harmonious filmic work instead of filmatized theater.

As regards the mentally sick Johannes, the play shows a complex of diseases, that is to say, a group of symptoms characteristic for various forms of mental disease which is quite common too. Diagnoses of mental sickness hardly ever show pure types of diseases. Johannes suffers clearly enough from delusions of greatness, as he believes that he is Jesus Christ. He has hallucinations and hears voices. When associating with other people, he is at the same time open and reserved. His behavior is more often characterized by dignity and sublimity. His speech is well considered, with a slight indication of preaching, bristling with quotations from the Scriptures and religious phrases, and his answers are both logical and coherent, at least superficially seen. As said before, he hallucinates, but in a very quiet way, and it has therefore been possible to keep him on the farm.

The clothes Johannes is wearing are loose-hanging, worn, and faded.

A psychiatrist would probably characterize his disease by the terms *megalomania, depression,* and *melancholy* and believe that the disease was provoked by excessive religiosity in connection with overwork owing to the theological studies, which, combined, caused a religious crisis. It is possible that Johannes fled into the disease partly as a protest against the studies, which were half-enforced on him, and partly for fear that he could not fulfill his father's expectations.

As an explanation of Johannes's sickness, it is not necessary to tell the story about his love affair and his fiancée's violent death. If this story too had to be included, it would have to be told in pictures, which would mean an unnecessarily heavy burden, and it would ruin the unity of space and (approximate) time which gives the plot a harmony and strength which must be preserved at any cost in the film.

The purpose of the film is to make the audience tacitly accept the idea of the author—such as it is experienced in the latter part of the film—namely, that the one who is strong enough in his faith also possesses the power to make miracles.

The audience must slowly be prepared for this purpose; they must get into a religious mood, be entangled into an atmosphere of religious mysticism. In order to make them receptive to the miracle, they must be brought into a special mood of sorrow and sadness which people have when attending a funeral.

When brought into this state of fear and contemplation, the audience will more easily get into a stage of being suggested to believe in the miracle, for the one reason that they—when being compelled to think of Death—are also coming to think of their own death and therefore (unknowingly) hope for the miracle and thus cut off their normal, skeptical attitude.

The audience must forget that they see a film and be put into a state of being suggested, or, if you prefer, so being hypnotized, to believe that they see a divine act, so that they walk away, silent and moved.

B Plot Summary of *Ordet*

This is a modified version of the official plot summary from the publicity developed by Palladium Studios.

Although *The Word* deals with a miracle, it is through and through a realistic film—about those who are weak in faith. The hoped-for miracle does not occur until one who has faith, the True Faith, arrives.

The action takes place among country folk living in a small, outlying parish on Jutland's west coast. It pictures the struggle between two different sides of Christian faith—a bright, happy Christianity and its contrast, a dark fanaticism, hostile to life.

The bright faith we find on a large old farm known as

Borgensgaard. The dark faith is in the modest home of the village tailor, where the gloom-sayers assemble for devotional meetings.

Borgensgaard's owner is old Morten Borgen, who has worked for the encouragement of the cheerful, life-affirming Christianity; many look up to him as their spiritual leader. But now doubt has begun to steal upon him: sorrow and disappointment have prepared the way. He has lost his wife, and of his three sons, the one to whom he was most deeply attached and of whom he expected the most is suffering from mental derangement. All three of his sons live on the farm.

The oldest son, Mikkel, works the farm. He also has caused his father grief; he does not share in the old man's belief. His wife, Inger, tries to convert him, but in vain. However, she satisfies herself by knowing he is a good and honest husband who loves her and their two little girls. She is expecting their third child—which they both earnestly hope will be a boy.

The next son, who is of unsound mind, is Johannes. His father encouraged him to study theology in the hope that he would carry on the religious traditions of the home. But the intensity of his religious studies causes a religious crisis and a nervous breakdown, ending in a mental disease. He now believes he is the Christ. His talk is nebulous, and he makes frequent use of quotations from the Gospels.

The youngest son, Anders, also causes his father grief because he has fallen in love with the very young Anne, daughter of the village tailor. Things are not easy for these two young people because they know all too well the implacability of their fathers. Encouraged by his brother Mikkel,

Anders has made up his mind to take the bull by the horns. He will go have a serious talk with Peter Tailor while Inger, his sister-in-law, promises to plead on his behalf with old Borgen.

Neither Anders nor Inger succeeds. Peter Tailor refuses to accept the connection between his pure and innocent daughter Anne and Anders, son of that heathen at Borgensgaard—and he shows Anders the door. Inger has fought hard against her father-in-law's country pride and his strong contempt for the "gloom-sayers" who gather at Peter Tailor's home.

Nevertheless, Morten Borgen is nearly at the point of succumbing to Inger's persuasions. Then Anders returns home from his unsuccessful offer of marriage. In a broken voice, he relates the disastrous defeat. When Morten Borgen learns that his son has been rejected by Peter Tailor—who ought to count himself lucky to be related to the people at Borgensgaard—his pride again takes hold. He orders Anders to drive with him to Peter Tailor's, declaring that Anders will get his Anne, just as sure as Morten's name is Morten.

The old man and his young son arrive just as Peter Tailor has called his flock together for a devotional meeting. Not until the meeting is finished can the two men talk.

Although old Borgen proceeds cautiously, Peter Tailor is not to be swayed. In his opinion, his daughter would become a "child of sin" the day she might move to Borgensgaard as the wife of Anders. There is a stormy scene between the two stubborn men: faith against faith. When the altercation reaches its highest point, the telephone rings. It is a message from Borgensgaard: Inger is in birth pangs, and it is feared her life is in danger. Peter Tailor is triumphant. God has put to the test those who will not bend to God's will. Morten Borgen loses his head because Peter wishes for the death of Inger. Unable to control his anger, he hits the tailor and leaves this "haunt of the gloomy men."

At Borgensgaard, there is apprehension and despair. The child, so fervently wished for, was born dead—and the mother has lost so much blood the worst is to be feared. At first, it looks as if Inger may survive, but then her condition changes, and she quietly slips into death.

When Mikkel brings the message that his wife has died, the insane Johannes quotes Jesus's words: "She is not dead, she only sleeps." He enters the death chamber. Just as Jesus raised the daughter of Jairi from the dead, he attempts to call Inger back to life but fails because he has forgotten to beg God for the power, without which miracles are not possible.

Instead of conquering death, Johannes falls into a death-like faint. His brothers carry him away. When he awakens from his faint, he sneaks away from the farm and hides himself.

The day before the burial, a funereal solemnity takes over at Borgensgaard. The coffin containing the lifeless Inger is in the best parlor; only the clergyman and the nearest relatives are permitted to say good-bye to her there. In the other rooms, the inhabitants of the parish have gathered together to express their sympathy. Inger was loved by all. The last comers—Peter Tailor, his wife, and daughter—arrive and walk straight into the best parlor because Peter Tailor has come for a reconciliation with Morten Borgen. As proof of his sincerity, he makes what is to him the ultimate sacrifice: he permits his daughter Anne to marry Anders.

Just as the order is given by old Borgen to close the coffin, Johannes enters. Has he recovered his senses? He begins by reproaching those present for their lack of faith. Why have none of them prayed to God to give Inger back to them? He answers: because among the "believers," not a single true believer can be found! They all speak of wonders and miracles, yet no one believes in them. But now the others' lack of faith has weakened his faith.

The small hand of a child is put into his. It belongs to one of Inger's daughters. Johannes had promised to awaken her mother from death, and the child's voice says: "You must hurry!" The child's faith in him gives Johannes his own faith back, and he steps forward to the coffin. Johannes prays to God to give him the Word—the creative, life-giving Word.

And to the dead, Johannes says: "In the name of *Jesus Christ*, as God wills it, return to life. I say unto you, 'Woman, arise.'" Inger opens her eyes and sits upright in the coffin. She lives. The miraculous has happened because nothing is impossible for one who positively believes.

Appendix

 Letters from Denmark

CARL TH. DREYER
81 Dalgas Boulevard
Frederiksberg F.

September 26th, 1955

Dear Jan,

I thank you for your letter and for your sending me the first half of your book for my consideration. I appreciate very much this act of friendship.

According to your wish I have made some corrections and crossed out some sections particularly in the part treating your being at Vedersø. I do so partly because some scenes you describe do not appear in the final film, partly because you in this part give so many details interesting to you who little by little became one of ours, but uninteresting to those who some day are going to read your book. And I did so for your sake as well as my own sake.

I think you ought to mention that the actress who played the part of Inger and in the film should give birth to a child in fact was pregnant in life and actually gave birth to her own child in the middle of the film, so when she came back from the clinic and was to make the child-bed scene she knew what it was all about.

I am now going to answer all your questions.

"In a lens darkly" is an excellent title, only if I were you I should omit the title of Sheridan le Fanu's book.

The plan and composition of your book is excellent too, not too dry or skeleton-like. Easy to read.

As to the person of Christ: I do not see him at all, but the first time I happen to meet him I'll know it is HE!

I intend doing the Jesus-film in color—and for wide-screen—and for CinemaScope if wanted.

I am of course at liberty to end the account of the life of Jesus wherever it pleases me: after the trial before Pilate, after the crucifixion, or after the resurrection. To me it seems most logical to end the film with the crucifixion. According to Isaiah!

My "floating shots"? Well, we have a lot of "floating close-ups" in this film [Ordet], some of them to a length of 5–6–7–8 minutes, or 800–1,000 feet long. This method of course gives a rhythm different from the rhythm of a scene cut up in 20–30 close-ups. The "floating close-ups" demand a precise camera-car-work and careful rehearsing.

Is there any item I particularly want you to include in

the book? Yes, I am a little sorry that you do not mention my film made in Berlin [about 1921]: *The Stigmatized* [based on Danish author Aage Madelung's fine novel *Elsker hverander*].

The French "réalisateur" is positively better than both the American-English "director" and the Danish "instruktør."

I shall be pleased if you'll use my essay on color films as an appendix, but in that case you ought together with it publish not only my essay "On Film-Style" [printed in *Films-in-Review* 1, no. 3 (January 1952)] but also the lecture I gave at the Edinburgh Festival on the 30th of August: "New Impulses in Film." In fact the three treatises complete each other. The lecture has the same length as the two others. If you are interested, please let me know, and I shall send you a typewritten copy in the English language.

I have no connection with de Rochemont or any other company.

I saw Blevins Davis a few weeks ago in London. He is interested more than ever in making the Jesus-film, so I hope very soon to go to Israel and start the preparatory work that has to be done down there. By the way: before you give your book to a publisher, please kindly send a copy to Mr. Davis—or authorize me to give him my copy to read. He might possibly help you to a good publisher! The photo of Joan of Arc on the black background with the gray matting is fine. My photo is less good. Couldn't you instead take the drawing by Dorothy Lovell?

I am not in Rungsted this year. I went to Venice for two days and from there to Edinburgh. I have been all summer in Copenhagen. My wife, my daughter and son are at present in Spain. They have hired a house outside Barcelona. I shall certainly give my wife your regards. She remembers you very well and with sympathy.

The Spook Sonata? Well, of course it can be made, only I am afraid it is a little too early. Don't you think so? But in 4–5 years perhaps.

I thank you for the two subscriptions which you mention in your letter [*The Saturday Review of Literature* and *The Moving Image*].

I also thank you for your commentary on the new films.

Mr. and Mrs. Michael Weyl are about to leave Copenhagen. I have not seen them in a long time.

I thank you again for giving me the opportunity to read your script. It will be sent as an ordinary letter registered.

And now, with all good wishes and with my kindest regards.

Very sincerely yours
Carl Th. Dreyer

* * * * * *

CARL TH. DREYER
              Copenhagen, Feb. 8th 1957
Mr. Jan Wahl
2116 Potomac Drive
Toledo 7
Ohio
U.S.A.
Dear friend,
       I am glad you liked the book I sent for Christmas, and I

am looking forward to receive *Porgy*. I cannot make any definite date on the Charleston journey, since I do not yet know what Blevins Davis is planning. It is up to him to decide. If he thinks it wise to postpone the Jesus-film, I shall of course only be happy to go ahead with another production—and *Porgy* is as you know one of my favorite ideas.

As to *Ordet* you had better advise Rochemont to contact Blevins Davis.

I thank you for the two nice cuts from my Joan of Arc film. It was indeed very sweet of you to put them on your letter as an ornament.

Sincerest wishes
Carl Th. Dreyer

* * * * * *

CARL TH. DREYER
18th April 1959
My dear friend,

In fact, I was a little surprised as I read in the papers that you had arrived in this country to work as secretary for Karen Blixen, and that I didn't get a single word from you. We were expecting you, and we should have been very pleased if we had seen you here at home. Now everything is explained and we cannot do anything but express our sympathy.

We are glad to hear that you have a very exclusive publisher, Macmillan, interested in your novel and that another publisher is interested in your poetry. As for your film book I hope it will become a palpable reality.

Since you in a very friendly way ask me if the idea is acceptable to me and if I mind your setting me up against the two others (Murnau and von Stroheim) I shall frankly tell you that I am not very enthusiastic about this line. Since the three of us in my opinion have nothing at all in common. I should very much have preferred to be put together with Elia Kazan and Ernst Lubitsch. With these two I know I have much in common and I am a great admirer of both of them. Or, if that doesn't satisfy you, then together with Seastrom and Mauritz Stiller. But since it is you who are going to write the book it is of course of importance what you personally feel about the matter.

Why do you bind yourself to just 5 films from each one? Isn't that a little artificial or rather little haphazard? Why don't you just say to yourself, I'll concentrate on the essential traits of their individual art?

It seems to me that you are too hard on Charlie Chaplin. On my part I was very happy to see *Monsieur Verdoux* because I in this film saw signs of an artist looking for new ways, for a new style and for a new outlook for his artistic imagination. I enjoyed all what was new in the film and I disapproved when he fell back on his old-time gags. *The King of New York* I have unfortunately not seen but I feel it is likely that Chaplin will give us another great film in which he has entirely disengaged himself from his former style.

As to my future plans Mr. Kay Harrison, the European president of Technicolor who also is interested in the Jesus-film, has some months ago made the suggestion that I should make another film before this film, which I have accepted, and we are just now talking of a subject which is very close to my heart.

My lovely wife sends you her best wishes and so do I— hoping soon to meet you somewhere.

Most sincerely
Carl Th. Dreyer

* * * * * *

CARL TH. DREYER
Copenhagen F.
March 29th, 1965
Dear Jan Wahl,

I thank you much for your nice little book, *The Beast Book*! What are you doing now? Anything with film?

Would it be possible for you to send me a single copy of your *Beast Book*? To be paid for, of course. I know a little girl who would be happy for it.

With best regards
Affectionately
Carl Th. Dreyer
We hope to see you soon!

* * * * * *

CARL TH. DREYER
Copenhagen F. 20/5 1965
Dear Jan Wahl—

I thank you much for your letter of May 11th. I am glad

that you like the article by Elsa Gress. She has fought bravely for *Gertrud*.

The idea about Maria Callas is splendid, and she might be interested, because such a film will bear witness to posterity of her remarkable power as a dramatic actress. But will she be able to free herself from the theatrical services . . . for about a couple of months, or maybe less.

At any rate I must have an American producer behind me.

Please read the Spring number of *Sight and Sound*. There is a fine article on *Gertrud*.

I hope we shall meet at the Festival in New York.

Kindest regards

Very sincerely

Carl Th. Dreyer

* * * * * *

CARL TH. DREYER

Copenhagen F.

May 30th 1965

Dear Mr. Wahl,

Since my last letter I have been in touch with Paramount's Paris office. M. Henri Michaud to whom I mentioned your splendid idea with regard to the actress to play Medea. He seemed earnestly interested and would write the President about the matter. I shall of course keep you informed.

I thank you for the booklet *The Beast Book*. It will one

of these days be forwarded to one of my girl friends—5½ year old. Her name is Birgitte. Isn't it poetic?

She'll enjoy it.

My best regards
Sincerely
Carl Th. Dreyer

Appendix

 D Dreyer on color film

Color films have now been on the screens of the world for twenty years. How many of them do we remember for the esthetic pleasure they gave us? Two—three—four—five?

Possibly five—but probably not more.

Romeo and Juliet just manages to be among them—after Olivier's *Henry V* and Kinugasa's *Gate of Hell*. Olivier got his ideas for his color schemes from the illuminated manuscripts of the period. Kinugasa got his from the classical wood-engravings of his people.

Except for these three films there have been only attempts to accomplish things with color. These attempts are best exemplified by *Moulin Rouge*, where the smoke-filled room, right at the beginning, compelled admiration. The rest of the film, so far as color is concerned, was mediocre. Why? In other scenes the *réalisateur* did not have Toulouse-Lautrec to hold on to. Huston is a great *réalisateur,* but as a painter Toulouse-Lautrec was greater.

So, in twenty years' time there have been three or four esthetically satisfying color films. A modest yield.

Apart from the amusing and surprising color effects that are to be found in film musicals, a rather plain taste has dominated the use of color in moving pictures. This may be due to a fear to depart from the firm fundament of naturalism—firm, but boring. There can be poetry, of course, in the colors of daily life, but color film does not become art by even a sincere imitation of nature's own colors. When a film colorist is merely imitating nature, the audience is merely appraising how well or ill the colors came out.

Indeed, we have so often seen the grass green, and the sky blue, that sometimes we wish we could see a green sky and blue grass—just for a change. Also, there might be an intention of an artist behind it. Let us not forget that color in film can never look exactly like the colors of nature. The reason is simple: in nature, color nuances are endless, and the human eye cannot distinguish them all from one another.

The tiny color differences, the semi-tones, all those nuances the eye receives without discrimination, are missing in color films. To demand that color in color films should be natural is to misunderstand all that is involved. Indeed, the spectator can have a much greater esthetic experience *because* color in film differs from that in nature.

Color is a valuable help to the *réalisateur.* When colors are chosen with due regard to their emotional effect, and selected to match each other, they can add an artistic quality to a film that black-and-white lacks. But it must always be borne in mind that color composition is as important in color film as composition in black-and-white.

In black-and-white films light is set against darkness, and line against line. In color films surface is set against surface, form against form, color against color. What the black-and-white film expresses in changing light and shade, in the breaking of lines, must, in color film, be expressed by *color constellations*.

There is also the matter of rhythm. To the many other rhythms in films, it is necessary now to add the color rhythm.

While a color film is being made the problem of how it will be cut—i.e., edited—must be a constant concern. The slightest shift can change the balance between the color planes and cause disharmony.

It must never be forgotten that because persons and objects constantly move in moving pictures, the color in color films constantly slides from one place to another in changing rhythm, and, when the colors collide, or melt together, very surprising effects can occur. The general rule about this is: use the smallest possible number of colors, and use them in conjunction with black and white. Black and white are too little used in color films. They have been forgotten in the childish rapture over the many bright colors in the paint-box.

All this makes the *réalisateur*'s task more difficult—and more attractive too. Creating a scene in black-and-white is a fight, as every *réalisateur* of integrity knows. Colors do not make the fight easier, but they do make the victory, when won, sweeter. And the victory will be much bigger when he succeeds in breaking the vicious circle which confines color films to naturalistic ideas. The color film can be a really great experience—in regard to colors—when it has been freed from the embraces of naturalism. Only then will the colors have a chance of expressing that which can only be perceived. Only then can the moving picture encompass the world of the abstract, which, hither to, has been closed to it.

The *réalisateur* must not see his pictures in black-and-white first and *then* think of color. The colors for the scenes must be in his mind's eye from the beginning. He must *create* in colors. However, color feeling is not something one can learn. Color is an optical experience, and the capacity to see, think, and feel in colors is a natural gift. We may presume that painters, in general, have that gift.

If there are to be more than just four or five artistic color films in the next twenty years, it will be necessary for the film industry to get assistance from those who can help—that is to say, from painters, just as the film industry has had to get help from authors, composers, and ballet masters. The *réalisateur* of a color film will have to add a painter to his already large staff, and the painter, in cooperation with, and responsible to him, must create the color effects of the film. A "color script" should parallel the actual script, and the painter's drawings in this "color script" should abound with details.

People may object: the *réalisateur* has his color technicians. These advisors are, and will undoubtedly remain, immensely useful to him, for their knowledge of chromatology and color theories can save him from many traps. But, with all respect to their efficiency and sense of responsibility, a good painter has one important quality they do not: he himself is a creative artist and fetches impulses from his own artistic mind. Incidentally, it will help the color technicians also to have a professional painter at hand.

Let us take a purely hypothetical case. Suppose Toulouse-Lautrec were alive and had worked on *Moulin Rouge* from the beginning to the end, not merely during the opening scenes, but in all the scenes. Wouldn't these then have been at the same high level as the opening scene, which was based on an actual color composition by Toulouse-Lautrec? And would not *Moulin Rouge,* instead of being a promising attempt, have turned out to be a really great color film? The *réalisateur* would not have been lessened thereby. It is not his job to do everything himself, but to guide everything, and keep it all together and force the parts into an artistic whole.

The wish underlying what I have written here is for the color film to get out of the backwater in which it is and sail forth on its own. As it is now, the color film seems to aim no further than to "look like" something it is not. *Henry V* tried to resemble a medieval illuminated manuscript, and *Gate of Hell* a Japanese print.

It would be ever so beneficial for there to be a color film which bore throughout the hallmark of a colorist of today. Then the color film would no longer be mere film with colors, but an alive art.

Appendix

E Dreyer's lecture at Edinburgh: "New Impulses"

We can all probably agree that the film of today is not perfect. But we can only be grateful for this as there is a chance of development in the imperfect. The imperfect is alive. The perfect is dead, pushed aside, we do not see it. But a thousand possibilities are open for the imperfect.

Film as an art stands in an era of struggle, and one is looking to see where the new impulses will be coming from. Because I actually used the term *new impulses* you naturally now expect a long, profound lecture with learned analyses and all that, but I will have to disappoint you. I am not a film theorist, unfortunately not—I do not have the brains for that. I am only a film director, and proud of my craft. But a craftsman too will get his own ideas during his work, and I would like to share these simple thoughts with you.

I do not have anything revolutionary to say. I do not believe in revolutions. They push development backwards. I am more inclined to believe in evolution, in the small steps forward. So I only intend to point out that film has possibilities of giving an artistic renewal from *inside.*

Human beings follow the principle of inertia, and are opposed to be taken away from the beaten track. They have by now got used to the correct photographic reproduction of reality and sure feel a certain happiness in recognizing what they already know. When the camera appeared, it won a quick victory because it in a mechanical way and objectively could register the impressions which the human eye sees.

This capacity has so far been the strength of the film, but as regards artistic films it is becoming a weakness we have to fight. We have got stuck with photography and now are confronted with the necessity of freeing ourselves from it. We must use the camera to drive away the camera.

We must work so that we are no longer slaves of the photography, but make ourselves masters of it. From being a purely reporting media photography should be turned into a tool for artistic inspiration, and direct observation be left to the sightseeing of film news.

Photography as a means of reporting has compelled the film to stand with its feet on the ground, and so it became addicted to naturalism. But not until the film has cut off its earth connection will it be able to fly into the sphere of imagination. So we have to wrench the film out of the embrace of naturalism. We have to define to ourselves that it is a waste of time to copy reality. By means of the camera we must give the film a new language of style and create a new artistic form.

But first of all we have to understand what we mean by the terms *art* and *style*. The Danish author Johannes V. Jensen characterizes *art* as a "spiritually interpreted form," and this can probably not be said any better. The British philosopher Chesterfield thinks that *style* is "the dress of thoughts." This definition is also simple and precise, presuming "the dress" is not too conspicuous, as the characteristic of a good style must be that it enters into such an intimate contact with the material that it forms a synthesis.

If it is pushing, so as to attract all attention, it is no longer *style* but *mannerism*. I myself would define *style* as "the form in which artistic inspiration expresses itself," because we recognize the style of an artist in certain features which are characteristic for him, and which reflect his mentality and personality in his work.

The style of an artistic film is a result of many different components, such as the playing of rhythms and lines, the mutual tension of the colour surfaces, the interaction of light and shadow, the gliding rhythm of the camera—all this, which combined with the director's conception of the material as a picture-creative factor, will decide his artistic form of expression—his style. If he confines himself to give a soulless, impersonal photography of what his eyes can perceive, he has no style. But if he uses his own mind to transform what his eyes saw, into a vision, and if he builds up his film in accordance with his vision, disregarding the reality which inspired him, then his work will bear the sacred stamp of inspiration, and then the film has a style, because style is the stamp of a personality put on a work.

When I entered the rostrum I might have given you the impression of being a humble and modest man. It may therefore be embarrassing for you to hear from my own mouth that I am not. On the contrary. I am very arrogant, so self-conceited, indeed, that I dare say for myself and on behalf of my colleagues that the director must be the man who must and shall leave his hallmark on the artistic film.

This does not mean an under-evaluation of the poet's share, but even if the poet is a Shakespeare, the literary idea in itself will not make the film a piece of art. This can only happen if the director, inspired by the poet's material, in a convincing manner gives it life in artistic pictures. I do not underestimate the team-work made by photographers, colour technicians, and architects and so on, but inside his collective the director will be, has to, and shall remain the prime and inspiring power. The man behind the work. The one who makes the poet's work sound so that we listen, the one who makes feelings and passions flare so that we are moved and touched. He is the one who puts his stamp on the film with this inexplicable something, called style.

This is my conception of the director's importance—and responsibility. We now know what film style is. But we would also like to know what an artistic film is. Let us formulate the question this way. What other art form is most closely related to films? In my opinion it must be architecture, which is the most perfect art form, as it is not an imitation of nature, but has sprung out direct from human imagination.

The characteristic of noble architecture is that all details are so finely harmonized as to fit in with the whole so that no small detail, however small it may be, can be changed without giving the impression of a flaw in the harmony—contrary to the non-architectural house, where all measures and proportions are haphazard. Something similar applies to the films. Only when artistic elements of a film have been welded together to form such a firm composition that none of its units can be left out or changed without damaging the whole, only then can the film be compared to an architectural piece of art, and all those films which do not satisfy these strict demands are but boring and conventional houses, which we will pass by without even noticing them.

In the architectural film the director will take over the role of the architect. He is the one who, from his artistic outlook on life, coordinates the many different rhythms and tensions with the dramatic curves of the poem, together with the psychological modulations in the actors' expressions and gestures, tonality of the dialogues, and thereby imprints his style on the film.

And now we are coming to the crucial point. Where is the possibility for an artistic renewal of the film? I can only answer for myself and see but one way: *the abstraction*. And in order not to be misunderstood, I shall hurry up and give you a definition of the word *abstraction* as the expression of an art conception which demands that the artist shall abstract himself from reality, so as to strengthen the spiritual contents, where those are of a psychological or purely esthetic nature.

Or to put it even more concise: the art must describe inner and not outer life. We have to get away from naturalism and find ways and means to introduce the abstract in our pictures. The capability to abstract is the presumption for all artistic creation. The abstraction gives the director a chance of getting outside the fence with which naturalism has surrounded the film.

I want to point out some of the roads open to the director who wants to introduce the abstract element in his pictures. The closest at hand is called *simplification*. Every creative artist is confronted with the same task: to be inspired by reality and then move away from it in order to give his work the form the inspiration provoked.

The director must therefore be free to transform reality so that it becomes consistent with the inspired simplified picture left in his mind, because the director's esthetic sense must not give way to reality. On the contrary: reality must obey his esthetic sense. Art is not a reproduction but subjective choice, and the director will therefore only pick out what he deems necessary to get a clear and spontaneous general effect.

The simplification may also aim at making the idea of the picture more evident, and striking. The simplification must then aim at cleansing the motif of all the elements which do not support the idea. But with this simplification, the motif is transformed into a symbol, and with symbolism, we are well on our way towards abstraction, as the idea of symbolism is to work through suggestions.

The filmic reproduction of reality must be true but cleansed of unimportant details. It must also be realistic, but transformed in the director's mind so as to become poetry. The director shall not be interested in the things in reality but in the spirit in and behind the things. Realism as such is not an art. Realities must be forced into a form of simplification and abbreviation and in purified form emerge in a kind of timeless, psychological realism.

This abstraction through simplification and inspiration of the subject matter can be practiced by the director under modest forms in the rooms of the films. How many rooms without souls have we seen on the screen? The director may give his rooms a soul through simplification by removing all superfluous matters for the benefit of a few articles, which in one way or other are valuable as psychological witness of the personality of the inmate, or as a characteristic feature showing his relation to the idea of the film.

Colours, of course, are so much, much more important means to obtain abstraction. Everything is possible with them, however, not until it has been possible to break the chain which still binds the colour film to the photographic naturalism of the black-and-white film. In the same way, as the French Impressionists were inspired by the classical Japanese woodcut artists, there is every reason for Western film directors to learn from the Japanese film *Gate of Hell*, where colours actually fulfill their purpose. I am inclined to believe that the Japanese themselves consider this film as a naturalistic film, true enough, with historical costumes, but still naturalistic.

Seen with our eyes, it seems like a style-film with a tendency toward the abstract. Only in a single scene does pure naturalism break through altogether, namely, in the scene with the tournament in the open, green plain. The style is broken for a few minutes, but the feeling of uneasiness is quickly forgotten over the beauties which the rest of the film gives us. The colours have undoubtedly been chosen according to a well-prepared plan.

The film tells us at least a lot, not only as regards colour composition and the rhythm which is so well known from the classical Japanese woodcuts but also about a constellation of warm and cold colours, and about the use of deep-going simplification, which is the more striking here because it is supported by the colour. *Gate of Hell* should encourage Western directors to use the colours more deliberately and with greater boldness and imagination. So far, the colours in most Western films have been used much too casually, and according to a naturalistic recipe.

We are at present moving on cats' paws. When getting real wild, we will throw about pastel colours, pink and light-blue, in order to prove that we at least have some taste. But as far as the abstract film goes, it will not be enough to have taste. Artistic intuition and courage are needed to select and compose contrast colours, which will back up the dramatic and psychological contents of the film.

The colours offer the great, nay, the greatest possibility of renewing the artistic resources of the film, and it is a pity that colour films have existed for twenty years and during this period of twenty years we can remember three to five films only whose colours gave us an esthetic experience. And the best one came from Japan. Let us learn from the Japanese. Others have done so, for instance, your famous countryman James Whistler.

While speaking about colours, which in themselves hold unlimited possibilities for abstraction, there is one more factor worth mentioning, because it may inspire to abstraction of a very special character. Photography presumes, as you know, an atmospheric perspective, and this means that light and shadow fade toward the background. There may be an idea there to obtain an interesting abstraction by deliberately eliminating the atmospheric perspective—or, in other words, give up the so much desired depth and distance effect. One should instead work towards an entirely new picture structure of colour surfaces all in the same plane so that they form one big, many-coloured surface in one, so as to eliminate the conception of foreground, middle distance, and background. In other words, get away from the picture with a perspective and adopt a pure surface effect. It is possible that very remarkable esthetic effects could be obtained in this way, probably well suited for films.

I hope I did not make you feel worried because I talked so much about "abstraction." It may sound like a naughty word in the ears of film people. What I wanted to say today was merely to point out that there is a world outside the gray and boring naturalism, namely, the world of imagination. This transformation must, of course, be made without the director or his helpers losing their hold on the world of realities.

Even if the director must remodel the world of reality to his artistic form, this changed reality must be presented in such a way that the audience will recognize it and believe in it. It is very important that the first attempts to introduce abstraction in the film are made with tact and discretion so that they do not shock people. It would be wise slowly to lead the audience into new roads. But should the attempts prove successful, then enormous prospects open up for the film. No task would be too high. The film may never become truly three-dimensional, but by means of abstraction, it may, on the other hand, be possible to introduce both a fourth and a fifth dimension in the film.

Now at last, I have talked so much about picture and form, and not a word about acting. But anyone who has seen my films—the good ones of them—will know how much importance I attach to the actor's performance. Nothing in the world can be compared to the human face. A land which one can never tire of exploring. A land with a beauty of its own, be it rough or wild. In fact, there is no greater experience than in a studio to witness how the expression of a sensitive face under the mysterious power of inspiration is animated from inside and turns into poetry.

Appendix

F Dreyer on film style

A work of art, like a human being, has a personality, a soul. It is revealed in the way the artist expresses his conception of whatever subject he treats. If the artist's inspiration is to be embodied in an artistic form, style is necessary. Through style the artist achieves unity, and through it he forces other men to see with *his* eyes.

Invisible and intangible, style permeates a genuine work of art and cannot be separated from it.

A work of art is always the outcome of the labor of a single man. But a motion picture is created by the exertions of a collection of men, and a collective cannot produce art unless an artistic personality gives the collective its energy and direction.

The first act in the creation of a motion picture is the author's, and his labor is the basis of the film. But thereafter all devolves upon the director, and it is he who forms the style of the film, who unites and brings to life the contributions of the individuals in the collective. The film becomes tinged with the director's feeling and sentiments. This must happen. Otherwise, in the hearts of the spectators, there will be alien moods, and merely personal reactions. It is the director's style that endows a film with a soul, that lifts it into the realm of art. The director alone can give a film a face—his own.

This is the director's great responsibility.

I would like to recount the things that determined the style of *Day of Wrath.** I shall commence by discussing the photography and the rhythm.

In talking pictures the spoken word too easily displaces the visual, actors are too garrulous, and the eye is infrequently invited to rest upon some fine, or some telling, pictorial effect. In *Day of Wrath* I attempted to restore to the visual the priority which is its due. But I did not introduce scenes merely for their pictorial beauty, merely to delight the eye. I adhered to the rule that unless a sequence advances the action it is detrimental to the picture. No matter how beautiful it may be.

Because bright tones in a picture lighten the mood of

Day of Wrath tells two stories simultaneously: the personal one of a young wife who falls in love with her stepson, and the social one of witchcraft and the suppression of the demonic forces called by that name.

the spectator and dark tones subdue it, my cameraman and I agreed that the historical period, and the story, of *Day of Wrath*, would be suggested best by slightly veiled photography, with soft gray and black tones.

Now the human eye easily accepts horizontal lines and reacts against vertical lines. The eye is diffident toward stationary things but is attracted by objects in action. Which is why the eye follows smooth and rhythmic panoramic camera movements with pleasure, and why, as a general rule, one must try to keep a picture in a continually flowing, horizontally gliding motion.

By the sudden introduction of vertical lines an immediate dramatic effect can be produced. For instance, the scene in *Day of Wrath* in which the ladder is raised prior to being thrown into the fire.

I come now to the question of rhythm.

In recent years there has been a conscious striving for a new rhythm, a special talking picture rhythm. I am thinking of certain American and of almost all the good French psychological films. In them the scenes were worth seeing and the lines worth hearing. In them there was a stability in the rhythm that makes it possible for the spectator to *repose* in the picture, while listening to the spoken words.

In *Day of Wrath* I strove for this rhythm. In some of the dramatic sequences (e.g., the two young people at Absalom's bier) I used, instead of rapidly changing pictures, what I would characterize as long, panoramic close-ups which rhythmically followed the actors, sensing their way from one actor to the other, depending upon which action was to be stressed next. In spite of, or perhaps because of, its almost

wave-length rhythm, this sequence is one of the passages that
affect the spectator most completely.

Day of Wrath has been aspersed as too ponderous and
too slow.

Quick rhythms can be very effective, but I have seen
films in which pictures were whipped by in an artificial
rhythm for the sake of blatant rhythm. Such rhythm is a ves-
tige of silent pictures, from which talking pictures are not yet
free. It is a relic from the time of the printed title. Between the
titles there was a void (the titles themselves were empty) and
the actors *rushed* through the pictures and the pictures *flew*
across the screen. There was rhythm in abundance.

I recall that when Victor Sjöström's *The Sons of Ingmar*
was first shown in Copenhagen more than a quarter century ago, the Danish producers shook their heads. Heavens!
Sjöström had the audacity to let his farmers walk as heavily
and sluggishly as farmers actually walk. It took quite a lot
of film to get them from one part of a room to another. The
Danish film world, of course, was wrong. Those Swedish
films, with their natural, lifelike rhythm, conquered the entire
continent of Europe. From them, all Europe learned—among
other things—that the rhythm of a film must derive from the
story and the setting, and that while the dramatics dictate
the rhythm, it is the rhythm that develops the mood in which
the drama is apprehended, and by which the reactions of the
spectator to the drama are influenced.

The complex story and the historical period of *Day of
Wrath* dictated the broad, restful rhythm for which we strove.

Now let me turn to drama.

In all of the fine arts we like to see representations of human beings, and to be shown their psychical reactions. This desire is intensified when we see people moving about on the screen. And though all of us are interested in action, and the overt acts of individuals, it is when we are taken into the realm of psychological conflict that we are really spellbound.

There is no lack of psychological conflict in *Day of Wrath*. It would be difficult to find a subject in which one could use so many superficial dramatics. But the actors, and myself (I dare add), chose not to be tempted. We battled against easy dramatic exaggeration, against dramatic clichés.

Is it not a fact that the greatest dramas occur in silence? Men hide their emotions, do not let their faces betray the storms raging in their souls. The tension beneath the surface is released only when a catastrophe occurs. The latent tension, the smouldering horror behind the everyday life of the vicarage, was what I tried to portray in *Day of Wrath*.

Some people thought I erred, and should have allowed a more violent development of the action. But if you observe your own friends, you will see how trivially, how undramatically, they experience the greatest tragedies. This, perhaps, is the most tragic part of tragedy.

There are also people who thought some sequences should have been more realistic. But realism, in and of itself, is not art. Only psychological realism is art—only the verity of life, liberated from all the irrelevance by the dedicated labor of a sincere artist. What takes place on the screen is not reality. Nor should it be, for then it would not be art.

Before continuing—I wish to define the difference between *theatrical* and *filmic*. As far as I am concerned, the word *theatrical* carries no derogatory connotation. I merely wish to point to the fact that an actor, of necessity, must act differently on a stage than in a film studio. On the stage he must be concerned that his words reach all the way up to the gallery. This requires not only a certain kind of diction and voice modulation, but also exaggerated mimicry. Film, however, requires ordinary speech, and natural mimicry.

In *Day of Wrath* we took pains to act with absolute verisimilitude. We warned each other against the gesture, the false emphasis. We revived natural mimicry.

When sound first came to film the importance of mimicry was forgotten, and for a time words poured out of empty faces.

Mimicry is vital to the motion picture, for mimicry acts upon our emotions directly, without any intervening intellectualization. It is mimicry that gives the soul a face, and one may read a man's whole character in a single piece of mimicry. Mimicry is the *primary* form of expression—prior to speech. Dogs are capable of a most expressive mimicry.

While discussing mimicry, I should like to mention makeup. Oddly enough, film actors usually make up for the photographer, who thereupon lights them in such a way that you do not see the makeup. Sophisticated audiences, however, have learned to appreciate the beauty of the natural face—with all its wrinkles and furrows. The wrinkles—small as well as large—are often clues to significant aspects of character. The face of a kind, smiling, hearty man develops minute wrinkles about the eyes and mouth. A sulky, dour, or malicious man gets frowns and vertical wrinkles. If these wrinkles are painted away, the characteristic features of the face also disappear, and I need not point out how this affects close-ups.

In order not to hide the least inflection of the mimicry in *Day of Wrath*, I used unpainted faces. It was a matter of course. It was in the very nature of *Day of Wrath* that the actors be unpainted.

It was also in the nature of this film that the actors should speak familiar language in an ordinary way.

A famous Danish actor, Carl Alstrup, was once asked if he would not like to play at the Royal Theater—the largest in Copenhagen. "No," he replied, "I can't shout my lines and still remain human."

Alstrup thereby revealed the difficulties an actor encounters on the stage, and the meaning of the word *filmic*. The film actor can keep his voice on its natural level—he may even *whisper* if the part calls for it. The microphone will certainly catch it and transport every word and pause.

For this reason, superfluous words must not be used in film. Speech must never be independent. It is an ingredient of a film—nothing more.

In choosing his actors, a director must pay great attention to their voices. It is important that they be attuned to each other and harmonize. In this connection, I would like to allude to something not generally known: there is an accord between the gait of a person and his speech.

I now come to the film director's most decisive task, that is, his collaboration with the actors.

The director is a kind of midwife. I think Stanislavski uses this metaphor in his *An Actor Prepares*. No metaphor could be more apposite. The actor is to bear a child, and it is the director's function to make things comfortable for the patient and to facilitate the delivery. The child, in every sense of the word, is the actor's—conceived, after a meeting with the author's words, from his own emotions and his innermost psychical life. It is always his own emotions that an actor gives to a part.

For this reason, a director gains if he does not force an actor to accept *his* interpretation. An actor cannot create true feelings by command. Emotions cannot be forced out of an actor. They must issue by their own force. The director and the actor should labor jointly to awaken them. When they succeed, the right expression will spontaneously arise.

For the sincere actor, the prime maxim is that he must never begin from the outside of his expression, but from the inside, from his emotions. But because emotion and expression are inseparably connected, are, in a way, a unity, it is sometimes possible to awaken the inner feeling by forcing an expression. Imagine an angry, sulking little boy amiably told by his mother: "Oh, smile a bit!" At first a stiff, awkward smile appears, then a more generous, open one, and finally he runs merrily about in high spirits. The first smile released feelings which influenced the subsequent expressions.

This interplay can sometimes be utilized by a director. If an actor is easily moved to tears (some are), it is wholly justifiable to allow him to melt into tears without awaiting the emotion that he is ultimately to feel and project. Ah, there is no satisfaction so delightful for director and actor as when the actor achieves the expression which he and the director know is right.

I cannot conclude this little essay on film style without mentioning music. It was Heinrich Heine who said that music carries on where words fail. Rightly employed, music both supports and deepens a mood engendered by picture and dialogue. If the music has real meaning and artistic intent, it will be an asset to the film. But we may hope—and strive to realize the hope—that the future will bring more and more films that have no need of music, more and more films in which the picture and the word do not fail.

I have now mentioned the technical and psychical processes which determine the style of a film. I admit that I have spoken much about technique. But I am not ashamed of having taken great pains to study my profession. Every artist knows that the prerequisite for true achievement is a thorough knowledge of his craft. Yet technique is the means, not the end.

The end is to enrich one's fellow human beings by engrossing them in emotional experience they would not otherwise encounter.

Filmography

Feature Films

The President (Denmark)

Danish title: *Praesidenten*
Production: Nordisk Films Kompagni, 1918
Script: Carl Th. Dreyer, from the novel by Karl Emil Franzos
Camera: Hans Vaagø
Sets: Carl Th. Dreyer
Cast: Halvard Hoff, Elith Pio, Carl Meyer, Olga Raphael-Linden, Betty Kirkeby, Richard Christensen, Peter Nielsen, Jacoba Jessen
Length: 5 reels
Premiere: February 1919, Stockholm; February 1920, Copenhagen

Leaves from Satan's Book (Denmark)

Danish title: *Blade af Satans Bog*
Production: Nordisk Films Kompagni, 1919

Script: Edgar Høyer, after Marie Corelli's novel *The Sorrows of Satan,* adapted by Dreyer
Camera: George Schnéevoigt
Sets: Carl Th. Dreyer
Cast: Halvard Hoff, Jacob Texiere, Erling Hansson, Hallander Hallemann, Ebon Strandin, Johannes Meyer, Tenna Kraft Frederiksen, Viggo Wiehe, Jeanne Tramcourt, Elith Pio, Carl Wieth, Clara Pontoppidan, Karina Bell
Length: 8 reels
Premiere: January 1921, Copenhagen

The Parson's Widow (Norway)

Swedish title: *Prästänkan*
Production: Svensk Filmindustri, 1920
Script: Carl Th. Dreyer, from the novel by Kristofer Janson
Camera: George Schnéevoigt
Cast: Hildur Carlberg, Einar Röd, Greta Almroth, Olav Aukrust, Kurt Welin, Emil Helsengreen, Mathilde Nielsen
Length: 6 reels
Premiere: October 1920, Stockholm; April 1921, Copenhagen

Love One Another (aka *The Stigmatized*) (Germany)

German title: *Die Gezeichneten*
Production: Primusfilm, 1921
Script: Carl Th. Dreyer, from the novel by Aage Madelung
Camera: Friedrich Weinmann
Sets: Jens G. Lind
Cast: Polina Piekovska, Vladimir Gajdarov, Torleif Reiss,

Richard Bolelavski, Dr. Duwan-Tovzov, Johannes Meyer, Adele Reuter-Eichberg

Length: 8 reels

Premiere: February 1922, Copenhagen; February 1922, Berlin

Once upon a Time (Denmark)

Danish title: *Der Var Engang*

Production: Sophus Madsen, 1922

Script: Carl Th. Dreyer and Palle Rosenkrantz, after the fairy tale by Holger Drachmann

Camera: George Schnéevoigt

Sets: Jens G. Lind

Cast: Clara Pontoppidan, Svend Methling, Peter Jerndorff, Hakon Ahnfeldt-Rønne, Torben Meyer

Length: 6 reels?

Premiere: October 1922, Copenhagen

Mikaël (Germany)

Production: Decla Bioscop (UFA), 1924

Script: Carl Th. Dreyer, after the novel by Herman Bang

Camera: Karl Freund and Rudolf Maté

Sets: Hugo Haring

Cast: Benjamin Christensen, Walter Slezak, Nora Gregor, Robert Garrison, Greta Mosheim, Alexander Murski, Max Auzinger, Didier Aslan, Karl Freund, Wilhelmine Sandrock

Length: 7 reels

Premiere: September 1924, Berlin

Master of the House (Denmark)

Danish title: *Du Skal Aere Din Hustru*
Production: Palladium, 1925
Script: Carl Th. Dreyer and Svend Rindom, from Rindom's
     play *The Fall of the Tyrant*
Camera: George Schnéevoigt
Sets: Carl Th. Dreyer
Cast: Johannes Meyer, Astrid Holm, Karin Nellemose, Mathilde
     Nielson, Clara Schønfeld, Johannes Nielsen, Petrine Sonne
Length: 8 reels
Premiere: October 1925, Copenhagen

The Bride of Glomdal (Norway)

Norwegian title: *Glomsdalbruden*
Production: Viktoria-Film, 1925
Script: Carl Th. Dreyer, from stories by Jacob B. Bull
Camera: Einar Olsen
Cast: Stub Wiberg, Tove Tellback, Harald Stormoen, Alfhild
     Stormoen, Einar Sissner, Oscar Larsen, Einar Tveito, Ras-
     mus Rasmussen, Sofie Reimers, Julie Lampe
Length: 8 reels
Premiere: January 1926, Oslo

The Passion of Joan of Arc (France)

French title: *La Passion de Jeanne d'Arc*
Production: Société Générale de Films, 1927
Script: Carl Th. Dreyer, after the book by Joseph Deltiel
Assistants: Paul la Cour and Ralph Holm
Camera: Rudolf Maté

Sets: Herman Warm and Jean Hugo
Costumes: Valentine Hugo
Editing: Carl Th. Dreyer
Cast: Maria Falconetti, Eugène Silvain, André Berley, Maurice Schutz, Antonin Artaud, Michel Simon, Jean d'Yd
Length: 8 reels
Premiere: April 1928, Copenhagen; October 1928, Paris

Vampyr (France)

Production: Film-Production Carl Dreyer, Paris, 1930–1931
Script: Carl Th. Dreyer and Christian Jul, after the novella *In a Glass Darkly* by Sheridan LeFanu
Camera: Rudolf Maté
Sets: Herman Warm
Music: Wolfgang Zeller
Cast: Baron Nicholas de Gunzberg, Henriette Gérard, Jan Hiéronimko, Maurice Schutz, Rena Mandel, Sybille Schmitz, Albert Bras, N. Babanini, Jane Mora
Length: 7 reels
Premiere: May 1932, Berlin

Day of Wrath (Denmark)

Danish title: *Vredens Dag*
Production: Palladium, 1943
Script: Carl Th. Dreyer and Mogens Skot Hansen, after the play *Anne Pedersdotter* by Hans Wiers-Jenssen
Camera: Karl Andersson
Sets: Erik Aaes
Costumes: K. Sandt Jensen and Olga Tomsen

Music: Poul Schierbeck
Editing: Edith Schlüssel and Anne-Marie Petersen
Cast: Thorkild Roose, Lisbeth Movin, Sigrid Neiiendam,
    Preben Lerdorff-Rye, Albert Høeberg, Olaf Ussing, Anna
    Svierkier
Length: 10 reels
Premiere: November 1943, Copenhagen

Two People (Sweden)

Swedish title: *Två Människor*
Production: Svensk Filmindustri, 1944
Script: Carl Th. Dreyer and Martin Glanner, after the play
    Attentat by W. O. Somin
Camera: Gunnar Fischer
Sets: Nils Svenwall
Music: Lars-Erik Larsson
Editing: Carl Th. Dreyer and Edvin Hammarberg
Cast: Georg Rydeberg, Wanda Rothgardt, Gabriel Alw
Premiere: March 1945, Stockholm

The Word (Denmark)

Danish title: *Ordet*
Production: Palladium, 1954
Script: Carl Th. Dreyer, after the play by Kaj Munk
Camera: Henning Bendtsen
Sets: Erik Aaes
Costumes: N. Sandt Jensen
Music: Poul Schierbeck
Editing: Edith Schlüssel

Cast: Henrik Malberg, Emil Hass Christensen, Preben Lerdorff-Rye, Cay Kristiansen, Birgitte Federspiel, Ann Elisabeth Groth, Susanne Rud, Einar Federspiel, Sylvia Eckhausen, Gerda Nielsen, Henry Skjaer, Ove Rud, Hanne Ågesen, Edith Thrane

Length: 10 reels

Premiere: January 1955, Copenhagen

Gertrud (Denmark)

Production: Palladium, 1964

Script: Carl Th. Dreyer, after the play by Hjalmar Söderberg

Camera: Henning Bendtsen

Sets: Kaj Rasch

Costumes: Berit Nykjaer

Music: Jorgen Jersild

Editing: Edith Schlüssel

Cast: Nina Pens Rode, Bendt Rothe, Ebbe Rode, Baard Owe, Axel Strøbye

Length: 11 reels

Premiere: December 1964, Paris; January 1965, Copenhagen

Short Films

Good Mothers (Denmark)

Danish title: *Mødrehjaelpen*

Production: Nordisk Film Company for Dansk Kulturfilm and Ministerienes Filmudvalg, 1942

Script: Carl Th. Dreyer

Direction: Carl Th. Dreyer

Music: Poul Schierbeck
Narrator: Ebbe Neergaard
Length: 12 minutes

Water from the Land (Denmark)
Danish title: *Vandet Paa Landet*
Production: Palladium for Ministerienes Filmudvalg, 1946
Script: Carl Th. Dreyer
Direction: Carl Th. Dreyer
Music: Poul Schierbeck
Narrators: Henrik Malberg and Asbjørn Andersen
Length: 11 minutes

Country Church (Denmark)
Danish title: *Landsbykirken*
Production: Preben Frank-film for Dansk Kulturfilm, 1947
Script: Carl Th. Dreyer and Bernhard Jensen
Direction: Carl Th. Dreyer
Camera: Preben Frank
Music: Svend Erik Tarp
Commentary: Carl Th. Dreyer and Ib Koch-Olsen
Narrator: Ib Koch-Olsen
Length: 14 minutes

The Fight against Cancer (Denmark)
Danish title: *Kampen Mod Kraeften*
Production: Dansk Kulturfilm, 1947
Script: Carl Th. Dreyer and Professor Carl Krebs
Direction: Carl Th. Dreyer

Camera: Preben Frank
Music: Peter Deutsch
Narrator: Albert Luther
Length: 12 minutes

They Caught the Ferry (Denmark)

Danish title: *De Naaede Faergen*
Production: Dansk Kulturfilm for Ministerienes Filmudvalg,
    1948
Script: Carl Th. Dreyer, after the story by Johannes V. Jensen
Direction: Carl Th. Dreyer
Camera: Jørgen Roos
Length: 12 minutes

Thorvaldsen (Denmark)

Production: Preben Frank for Dansk Kulturfilm, 1949
Script: Carl Th. Dreyer and Preben Frank
Direction: Carl Th. Dreyer
Camera: Preben Frank
Music: Svend Erik Tarp
Narrator: Ib Koch-Olsen
Length: 10 minutes

Stormstrøm Bridge (Denmark)

Danish title: *Storstrømbroen*
Production: Preben Frank-film for Dansk Kulturfilm, 1950
Script: Carl Th. Dreyer
Direction: Carl Th. Dreyer
Camera: Preben Frank

Music: Svend S. Schultz
Length: 7 minutes

A Castle within a Castle (Denmark)

Danish title: *En Slot I Et Slot*
Production: Teknisk Film Co. for Dansk Kulturfilm, 1954
Script: Carl Th. Dreyer
Direction: Carl Th. Dreyer and Jørgen Roos
Music: Archives
Narrator: Sven Ludvigsen
Length: 9 minutes

Index